BY GREEN FIG

Prophets' Stories

History of the Most Noble Mission

Volume 2

DESIGN & ART BY

Guzel Murtazina

NOTE:

Pictures in this book
don't correspond to reality

Publisher: Green Fig
Pennsylvania, USA
gogreenfig.com
ISBN 978-1953836748 (pb)

CONTENTS

INTRODUCTION

Dear young readers, As-salamu 'alaykum!

If you are reading these lines now, it's time to embark on an exciting journey! This book recounts the lives of the best people on earth and the stories that happened to them. As you read, you'll not only discover fascinating details about the lives of the prophets but also find answers to questions, and perhaps, see the world that surrounds you in a whole new light.

The belief in the prophets is an integral part of Faith (Imān), as taught to us by our beloved Prophet Muhammad (مُحَمَّد) ﷺ.

Imān is:

1. Believing in Allah without associating partners with Him.
2. Believing in the angels, who never commit any sin and always obey Allah's commands.
3. Believing in the Holy Books.
4. Believing in the prophets sent to guide us and teach the truth.
5. Believing in the Day of Judgment, when humans and jinns will be judged.
6. Believing in Al-Qadar, which means that everything in this universe happens by the Will of Allah.

Allah is not a man, angel, or like anything else we can imagine. However, we can contemplate the traces of His Power. Look around, and you will see many amazing creatures, all created by Allah the Almightly! He created the heavens, the earth, and all of us. Additionally, Paradise and Hell were created by Him. Paradise is a place where believers will be rewarded for their faith and good deeds, while Hell is prepared for those who deserve punishment due to their bad deeds.

Allah has established rules and laws for us. By following these rules, we find true happiness. We all desire to reach Paradise and enjoy eternal happiness in the Hereafter. To achieve this, we must follow the path of the prophets.

Take the time to read each chapter carefully and remember these amazing stories.

We wish you a pleasant journey!

WHO ARE THE PROPHETS?

The Belief in the prophets is one of the foundations of Islam. Prophets are the best of all the creations. Allah the Almighty sent them to people to call to Islam. All the prophets taught people that this world has a creator—Allah, and that only Allah deserves to be worshipped. All the Prophets, without exception, were believers in the One God, and none of them associated partners with Him. All the Prophets were Muslims; they ordered people to do good deeds and forbade doing evil.

Among the prophets were the messengers to whom Allah revealed a new set of laws (Shari'ah); some of these laws differed from the ones revealed to the messenger before him. These laws determined what was permissible and what was forbidden and taught people how to live and do acts of worship correctly. They taught ablution, prayers, judgments about marriage and many other things.

All prophets, whether messengers or not, called people to Islam, received the revelation, and conveyed to others what they were ordered to convey.

To some prophets, Allah gave the Holy Books or Scriptures. These sacred books were revealed in different languages. There were 104 Books in total. The last of them is the Holy Qur'an revealed to our Prophet Muhammad ﷺ. The Qur'an will be preserved until the end of the world, while the previous books have been either distorted or not present anymore with people.

Family Tree of the 25 Prophets mentioned in the Qur'an

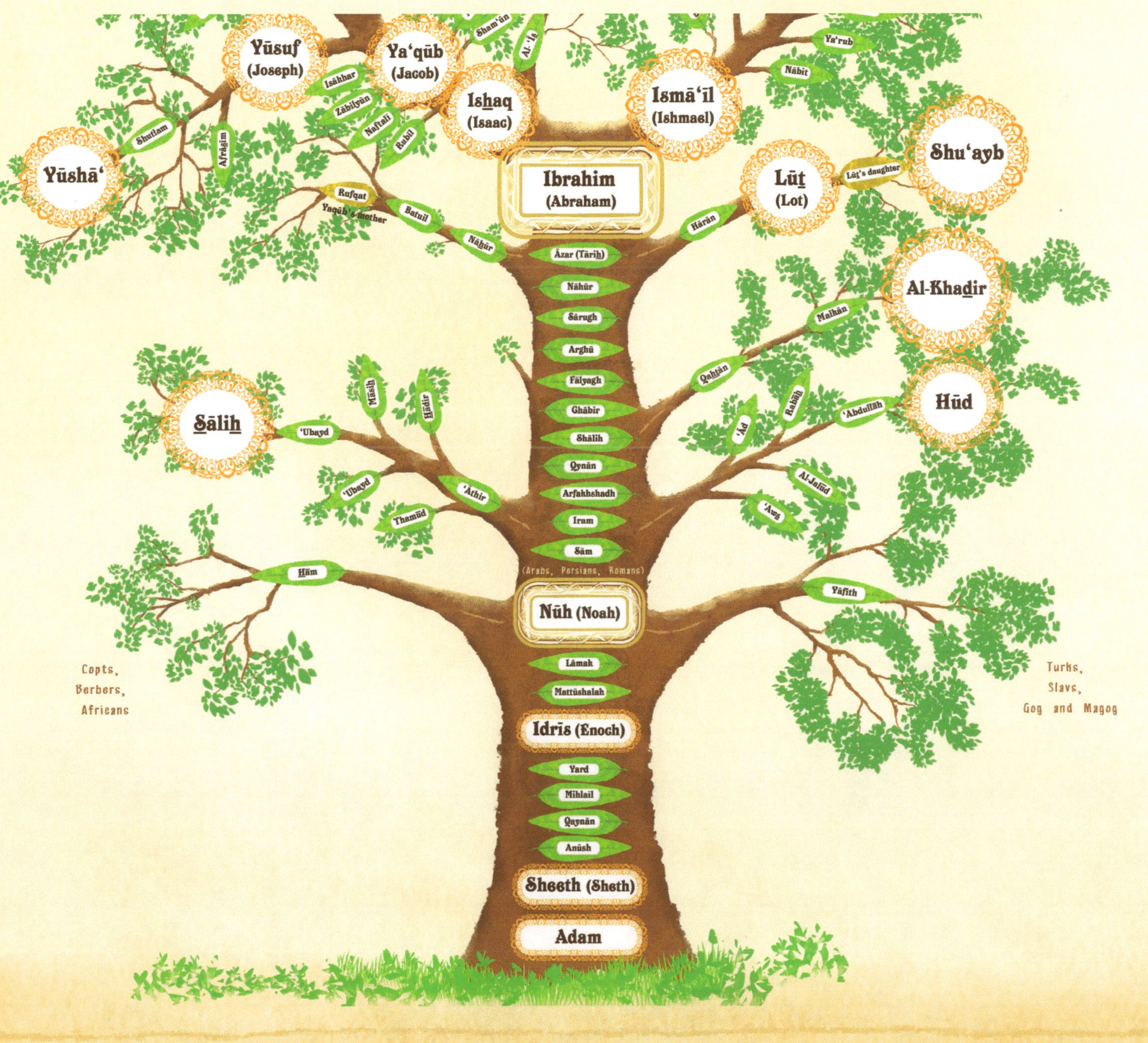

Family Tree of the 25 Prophets mentioned in the Qur'an

How Many Prophets Were There?

Throughout the history of humankind, there have been thousands of prophets, of whom 313 were messengers. We only know the names of some of them. The Holy Qur'an mentions the names of 25 prophets. The first prophet and messenger was Adam ﷺ, and the last was Muh̲ammad ﷺ, the best of all the prophets!

The prophets were people from different nations and spoke different languages, but they all called for One God and their religion was Islam.

Virtues of the Prophets

Allah entrusted the prophets with a special mission—to call people to the true religion and bring Shari'ah to them. This is a great and honorable work, and it is entrusted to the most worthy! Therefore, the prophets are the best creations of Allah and the most honorable of people. Allah the Almighty gave His chosen ones the most beautiful attributes. All prophets, without exception, were intelligent, sincere, honest, courageous, kind, generous, truthful and eloquent. They were never cowards, they never betrayed, and they never committed even the slightest meanness. All the Prophets were beautiful, with great manners because these attributes make them more attractive to people and more likely to be accepted by them. Allah gave all the prophets great miracles. A miracle is an extraordinary matter that proves the truthfulness of the prophet and cannot be challenged.

Prophets have always been believers (Muslims) even if they lived among unbelievers. They never worshiped anyone but Allah, and did not commit acts of blasphemy—neither before receiving the revelation of the prophethood, nor after. The Creator endowed his chosen ones with wisdom and patience. Allah also gave them great trials to show us the greatness of their character and their high status. Their life is an example for us and a support in life's difficult situations.

PROPHET YA'QŪB (JACOB) 

Prophet Ya'qub was the son of Prophet Is_haq and the grandson of Prophet Ibrahim ﷺ. Ya'qub's son, Yusuf, was also a Prophet. This is the only time in history where prophethood continued in four consecutive generations!

Another name of Prophet Ya'qub ﷺ is Israel, so his descendants are called "Banu Isra'eel" or Israelites.

Prophet Ya'qub ﷺ had a large family. He had twelve sons: Robil (Reuben), Sham'un (Simeon), Lawa (Levi), Yahuda (Judah), Isachar (Issacchar), Zabilun (Zebulun), Dan, Naphtali, Jad (Gad), Ashir (Asher), Yusuf (Joseph) and Binyamin (Benjamin). Yusuf and Binyamin were full siblings, sharing the same mother, Rahil (Rachel).

Mission of Prophet Ya'qub ﷺ

Ya'qub was born in Palestine, in the area of Canaan (Kan'an). He grew up in the house of his father, Prophet Is_haq ﷺ. Then for some time Ya'qub lived in the area of Harran where a maternal uncle resided.

Like all Prophets, Ya'qub ﷺ called people to Islam. He forbade idolatry and called for worshiping only Allah.

Allah tested Ya'qub ﷺ with many difficulties and trials in this life, elevating his status for his patience.

Death of Prophet Ya'qub ﷺ

Prophet Ya'qub ﷺ lived for more than 100 years. Like Prophet Ibrahim ﷺ, he advised his sons upon his death to firmly hold unto faith until death. Before passing away, Prophet Ya'qub ﷺ asked Yusuf to bury him next to his father Is<u>h</u>aq and grandfather Ibrahim. Yusuf fulfilled his father's request and buried him in Palestine, in the city of Hebron (al-Khalil), in the same cave where his father, mother, grandfather, and grandmother were buried.

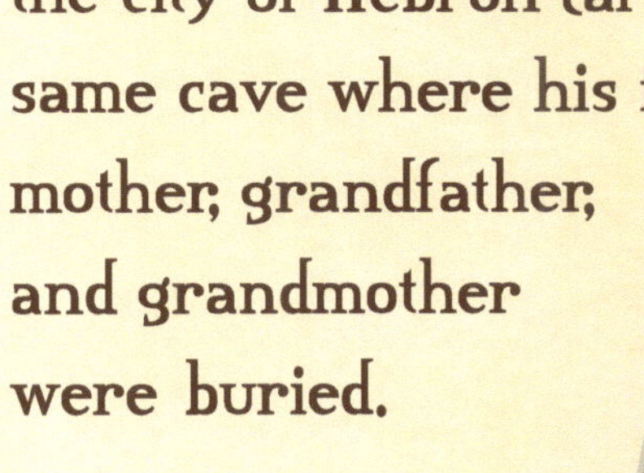

PROPHET YŪSUF ﷺ

Yusuf was the son of Prophet Ya'qub, the son of Prophet Is<u>h</u>aq, the son of Prophet Ibrahim ﷺ. Prophet Yusuf ﷺ was very God-fearing, chaste, patient, noble, kind and generous. He was extremely beautiful, Allah gave him half of the beauty distributed among humans on this earth!

Dream of Prophet Yusuf ﷺ

Ya'qub ﷺ had twelve sons. Prophet Ya'qub was fair to all his children; but he loved Yusuf and Binyamin more for their good character and kindness. The other brothers were jealous of Yusuf and Binyamin and harbored hatred in their hearts for them.

When Yusuf was twelve years old, he had a dream in which eleven stars, the sun, and the moon prostrated to him. When Yusuf told his father about his dream, Ya'qub ﷺ saw it as a sign indicating Yusuf's special status, and instructed him not to tell his brothers about it, fearing that they might harm him out of envy.

The brothers eventually found out about this dream. Their envy of Yusuf increased and led them to plan to separate Yusuf from his father, hoping that over time he would forget him and love them only. They said that after they do this, they will repent and become righteous people.

Conspiracy of Yusuf's Brothers

At first, Yusuf's brothers wanted to kill him or take him away from home so that he could no longer return. However, one brother, Judah, was against the murder of Yusuf. He said, "Do not kill Yusuf, but throw him into the well. Travelers passing by will find him and take him with them and you get rid of him." He made his other brothers promise not to kill Yusuf. Binyamin did not participate in the conspiracy against Yusuf. He had a pure heart, he did not commit any mean wrongdoing, and loved his older brother Yusuf very much.

To carry out their plan, the brothers went to their father and persuaded him to let Yusuf go with them to the countryside to play. Prophet Ya'qub ﷺ, knowing the hatred of Yusuf's brothers for Yusuf, did not want to let his beloved son go. He told them, "I am worried that you will leave Yusuf unattended and he will be eaten by a wolf." The brothers cunningly assured their father that they would take care of Yusuf and they were not afraid of a wolf as there were many of them and they were strong. Prophet Ya'qub ﷺ feared the brothers' hatred of Yusuf more than a wolf attack but he agreed to let his son go.

Once they were out of sight from their home, the brothers headed to a well. There, they hit Yusuf, took off his shirt and tied his hands. Then, the cruel brothers lowered Yusuf into the well. He landed on water, but did not drown since the water level was not high. He then climbed on a boulder in the well. Allah gave Yusuf the knowledge that he will be safe and that, one day, he will tell his brothers of what they did without them being aware who he is.

To hide their deed, Yusuf's brothers slaughtered a lamb and smeared its blood on Yusuf's shirt. They returned home when it was dark, sobbing loudly. Hearing their cry, Prophet Ya'qub ﷺ became alarmed. He asked them, "What's the matter with you, my children? Did something happen to your sheep?" They answered, "No." Prophet Ya'qub asked, "What happened? Where is Yusuf?" The brothers said, "Oh, our father! We left Yusuf near our stuff, and we ourselves went off to compete in racing and archery. We got too carried away and didn't keep track of him, and a wolf ate him. Truly, we speak the truth, even if you do not believe us!" Hearing this, Prophet Ya'qub ﷺ began to cry and asked, "Where is his shirt?" They showed him Yusuf's bloody shirt. Ya'qub took it in his hands and examined it carefully from all sides—there was not a single tear or hole in it! He said, hinting at their deception, "What a neat wolf! He ate my son without even tearing his shirt!" Guessing that they were hiding something, Prophet Ya'qub said, "You have committed great evil by succumbing to the temptations of the devil, but I will endure! I trust Allah, the Almighty, may He help me survive the loss of Yusuf. Verily, He knows what you hide."

Yusuf in the House of Al- 'Aziz

Yusuf stayed in the well for three days. A trade caravan passed by the well, and the merchants stopped near the well and sent one man to draw water. When he lowered the bucket into the well, Yusuf caught hold of the rope. Raising the bucket, this man saw a boy with a beautiful, radiant face. He exclaimed, turning to his companions, "Oh, what a joy! Look, there's a young boy!" His companions rushed to his help, and together they pulled Yusuf out. The brothers found out about this incident so they came to the merchants and told them that Yusuf was their runaway slave. They sold Yusuf to the merchants as if he was a slave, though he was not a slave. The merchants gave them little money for him, about twenty dirhams and continued their trip to Egypt.

In Egypt, the advisor of the King (vizier) known by Al-'Aziz or Potiphar purchased Yusuf. So Yusuf ended up in the house of a very rich and noble man who managed the state's economy and treasury. Al-'Aziz, who did not have any children, liked Yusuf and asked his wife Zalikha to treat him well. He told her, "Maybe he will be of benefit to us or we can take him as a son." In his house, Yusuf was surrounded by attention and care. Over time, Al-'Aziz saw that Yusuf was very knowledgeable, wise, and honest, and he made him his assistant, putting him in charge of the house and his servants. Yusuf lived in the vizier's house for several years.

When Yusuf grew up, he became such a wonderful young man. Zalikha, the beautiful wife of Al-'Aziz who raised him, felt in her heart an inclination towards him. One day, she closed the doors and said to Yusuf, "I am ready for you." He firmly refused her advances and said, "I seek refuge with Allah Indeed, the wrongdoers will never succeed."

وَرَاوَدَتْهُ الَّتِي هُوَ فِي بَيْتِهَا عَن نَّفْسِهِ وَغَلَّقَتِ
الْأَبْوَابَ وَقَالَتْ هَيْتَ لَكَ ۚ قَالَ مَعَاذَ اللَّهِ ۖ إِنَّهُ رَبِّي
أَحْسَنَ مَثْوَايَ ۖ إِنَّهُ لَا يُفْلِحُ الظَّالِمُونَ ٢٣

سورة يوسف

This means that the Lord of the worlds made Yusuf's manners good and protected him from falling into this sin. Moreover, Al-'Aziz entrusted him with what he had, and a prophet does not betray the trust.

All prophets are pure and chaste.
They never desire, intend, or commit sinful acts like adultery (having a forbidden intercourse with a woman) or engage in any actions that lead to it. It takes one out of Islam to attribute any of those things to any prophet.

When Zalikha tried to get closer, he thought of pushing her away to get rid of her, had it not been that he saw the evidence from his Lord. At that moment, it was revealed to Prophet Yusuf that if he shoved her away, she would say to her husband he pushed her to force her. And this is the meaning of the verse from the Qur'an:

وَلَقَدْ هَمَّتْ بِهِ وَهَمَّ بِهَا لَوْلَا أَنْ رَأَى بُرْهَانَ رَبِّهِ ﴿٢٤﴾

سورة يوسف

"She wanted to do the bad act with him, and he wanted to push her away from him had he not seen the proof from Allah."

So, Yusuf did not push her; rather, he pulled away from her and hurried towards the door to leave the room. She followed him back wanting to prevent him from leaving and grabbed him by the back of his shirt, causing the shirt to tear. They found her husband at the door who saw them in this situation. Zalikha quickly began to justify herself claiming that it was Yusuf who made advances. She demanded that her husband imprison Yusuf. Yusuf defended himself. It was her word against Yusuf's word. Allah Almighty made Yusuf's innocence appear. A baby from her family, whom Al-'Aziz used to favor and was present with him, spoke in an extraordinary manner and said, "Look, if Yusuf's shirt was torn from the front, then she is telling the truth, and he is lying. And if his shirt was torn from the back, then she is lying, and Yusuf is telling the truth." Hence, if his shirt was torn from the front, it means he attacked her and she resisted, while if his shirt was torn from the back it means he fled from her and she grabbed the back of his shirt. Seeing that Yusuf's shirt was torn from the back, Al-'Aziz knew that Yusuf is innocent and said to his wife: "Truly, this is from the deceit of women. Indeed, their deceit is great!" and then he told her, "Repent from your sin."

Al-'Aziz asked Yusuf not to tell anyone what happened. Nevertheless, the news still spread throughout the city. The women of the city began to gossip about Zalikha and how she had fallen madly in love with her servant. Having heard about this, Zalikha invited those women to her home. She offered them a lounge and food that needed to be cut with a knife. She gave each one a knife and offered them the food at the time when Yusuf was passing by. When the women saw Yusuf, they were so taken by his beauty to the extent that they stopped paying attention to what they were doing and cut their hands with the knives without even feeling the pain! Then Zalikha confessed everything and said, "This is the one you are blaming me for falling in love with. He spoke the truth. I did make unwanted advances, but he strongly refused. But if he does not do what I tell him, he will be punished and thrown into prison!"

قَالَتْ فَذَٰلِكُنَّ الَّذِى لُمْتُنَّنِى فِيهِ ۖ وَلَقَدْ رَٰوَدتُّهُۥ عَن
نَّفْسِهِۦ فَاسْتَعْصَمَ ۖ وَلَئِن لَّمْ يَفْعَلْ مَآ ءَامُرُهُۥ لَيُسْجَنَنَّ سورة يوسف
وَلَيَكُونًا مِّنَ الصَّٰغِرِينَ ﴿٣٢﴾

Then the women told him to obey Zaleikha, which of course he didn't. Yusuf chose prison, refusing to commit a forbidden deed.

Yusuf in the Prison

Despite knowing his innocence, Al-'Aziz imprisoned Yusuf at the request of his wife, hoping the incident and his wife's scandal would be forgotten. Yusuf found himself unjustly imprisoned but was very patient.

The people in the prison liked Yusuf and trusted him because of his great manners and high character. Two persons were imprisoned with him: one was the cupbearer to the king, and the other one was the king's baker. They were both accused of poisoning the king. One night, each saw a dream. One saw himself squeezing grapes, and the other saw that he was carrying bread on his head, and birds were pecking at it. They asked Yusuf for the meaning since they learned that Yusuf has the knowledge of interpreting dreams. Before doing so, Yusuf talked to them about something more important and called them to Islam. He told them, "These dispersed idols that you worship are not deserving of worship. Worship only Allah, who has no partner to Him in godhood. You do not worship instead of Him but names of idols that you have wrongfully

designated you and your fathers." Yusuf also showed them proofs of his truth by telling them what would their food be before it arrives. Then he interpreted the dreams, telling the one who saw himself squeezing grapes that he would be released and return to his work as a cupbearer, while the other would be executed in three days, put on a pole and his head would be eaten by birds. Everything happened just as Yusuf said.

Yusuf asked the one inmate whom he thought he would be released to tell the king about his unjust imprisonment. However, the man forgot, and Yusuf spent several years in prison.

The King's Dream

One day, the king of Egypt had an unusual dream that alarmed him. He saw in the dream seven large, well-fed cows emerge from the Nile River, followed by seven weak, skinny cows. The skinny cows ate the fat ones. He also saw seven green and seven dry ears of grain—the dry ears ate the green ones. The king asked his council for an interpretation but none could provide one.

It was then that the king's cupbearer remembered Yusuf, who had interpreted his dream while in prison. The man went to the prison and asked Yusuf about the king's dream. Yusuf ﷺ interpreted it as follows: "First there will be seven fruitful years. After that, there will be seven years of drought, during which people will eat what they stored during the harvest years."

The cupbearer returned to the king and shared Yusuf's interpretation. The king, surprised, ordered Yusuf to be brought to him. However, Yusuf first demanded that his innocence be known. He told the herald who came to take him to ask the king to find out about the women who cut their hands. The king summoned the wealthy women including Zaleikha. When asked, the women said, "We seek refuge with Allah. We know nothing bad about him." Then Zaleikha, the woman who wrongly accused Yusuf, admitted her plot and declared Yusuf's innocence. She said, "Now the truth is exposed, I wanted him but he refused. He is truthful."

قَالَتِ امْرَأَتُ الْعَزِيزِ الْآنَ حَصْحَصَ الْحَقُّ أَنَا
رَاوَدتُّهُ عَن نَّفْسِهِ وَإِنَّهُ لَمِنَ الصَّادِقِينَ ﴿٥١﴾

سورة يوسف

Afterwards, Yusuf left the prison and came to the king. The king asked for his advice and Yusuf ﷺ suggested sowing a lot of wheat over the next seven years and storing the harvest, using only what was needed for food. He taught them to store grains without separating them from the ears to prevent spoilage and advised building special warehouses for storage.

Seeing Yusuf's insight, wisdom and honesty, the king decided to make him one of his advisers. Yusuf was entrusted with controlling the flow of grain in the granaries and managing Egypt's treasury and food supply.

Call of Prophet Yusuf ﷺ to Monotheism

Allah gave Yusuf the Revelation when he reached his prime and commanded him to call the inhabitants of Egypt to Islam. While in the position of treasurer, Yusuf ﷺ with wisdom and gentleness called people to monotheism. The people of Egypt loved Yusuf for his wonderful qualities–kindness, mercy, generosity, and honesty. Many of them accepted Islam, including the king, seeing that it calls them to goodness and happiness.

The Drought

During the seven fruitful years, Prophet Yusuf ﷺ stockpiled food. He built warehouses for storing grain and made sure that only enough was used for food from the harvest, with the rest put into storage. After these years, a severe drought came that lasted seven years, and famine began. Prophet Yusuf ﷺ sold the people of Egypt exactly enough wheat to live on, but nothing more. Acting justly and wisely, he earned great respect, and his fame spread throughout many countries.

Yusuf's Meeting with his Brothers

It was a difficult time not only for Egypt, but also for neighboring territories. The people of Palestine also suffered from the drought. Having learned that there was a merciful and fair treasurer in Egypt, Prophet Ya'qub ﷺ sent his sons there to get food. Only Binyamin remained at home with his father. When the brothers

arrived in Egypt, they immediately went to Yusuf. Yusuf recognized them, but they did not recognize him! After all, before them was the chief treasurer of Egypt, and they could not even imagine that it could be their brother Yusuf!

Now Yusuf had wealth and power, but he did not take revenge on his brothers for the suffering they caused him. Prophet Yusuf ﷺ received them well and was kind and generous with them. He gave the brothers food—as much as was due for each person.

He did not see Binyamin among the brothers. To find out about him, Yusuf began to ask them who they are and how many brothers there are in total. They told him, "We were twelve brothers, but one brother left us, and his brother (on his father's & mother's side), Binyamin, stayed with our father." They told Yusuf that their father did not let Binyamin go with them because he loved him very much and was worried about him. Then Yusuf said, "Next time, bring your brother with you and do not be afraid—because you see that I received you well. And if you arrive without him, you will not receive food." The brothers promised that they would try to persuade their father to let Binyamin go with them.

Yusuf was worried that perhaps next year they would no longer have enough money to pay for the wheat and then they would not be able to come again. Therefore, he ordered his assistants to quietly put back into the brothers' belongings the goods by which they had purchased the food.

Return of Yusuf's Brothers to Palestine

The brothers of Prophet Yusuf returned to their father Prophet Ya'qub, their camels loaded with food. They spoke of the generous treasurer of Egypt who received them very well. They told their father that he told them to bring their younger brother Binyamin with them next time; and if they do not fulfill this request, then they should not come, as he will not give them food. The brothers began to beg their father to let Binyamin go with them next year, but Prophet Ya'qub did not agree, telling his sons, "I cannot entrust Binyamin to you, because you once promised to take care of Yusuf, but did not keep your word!"

When the brothers of Prophet Yusuf ﷺ opened the packs that they had brought from Egypt, they discovered that the silver with which they had paid had been returned to them. They took advantage of this to persuade their father to let Binyamin go with them. They said: "Oh, our father! What more could we wish for?! We were given food and our goods were returned. If you let Binyamin go with us, we can go there again and bring food for our family and people. Don't worry, we'll make sure nothing happens to him on the way. Besides, if there are more of us, we will bring even more food, because food is given for each person."

Prophet Ya'qub did not want to let Binyamin go. After all, he loved him very much. However, since there was a very severe drought in Palestine and people were suffering from hunger, Prophet Ya'qub agreed to let Binyamin and his brothers go, taking an oath from them that they would protect him with all their might and return with him.

Yusuf and Binyamin

The next year, Yusuf's brothers went to Egypt again to buy food. This time, as Yusuf demanded, they took Binyamin with them. Prophet Yusuf again received them very well. He prepared food and drinks for them and set the table so that the guests sat in groups of two. All the brothers sat down two by two, and Binyamin was left alone. With deep sadness in his heart, he said, "If my brother Yusuf were alive, he would be sitting next to me." Yusuf heard Binyamin's words and said to the other

brothers, "I see that your brother is left alone, so let him sit with me." When evening came, Yusuf prepared a place for the guests to sleep in such a way that the brothers slept in twos. And when Benyamin was left without a partner again, Yusuf said: "He will sleep with me." When Yusuf was alone with Binyamin, he asked him, "Do you have a brother on your father's and mother's side?" Binyamin replied, "I had a brother, but he died." Then Yusuf revealed himself to him and said, "Truly, I am your brother Yusuf! Do not be sad because of the evil that our brothers have done to us." Then he asked Binyamin not to reveal this secret to his brothers and said that he would make sure that Binyamin stayed with him in Egypt.

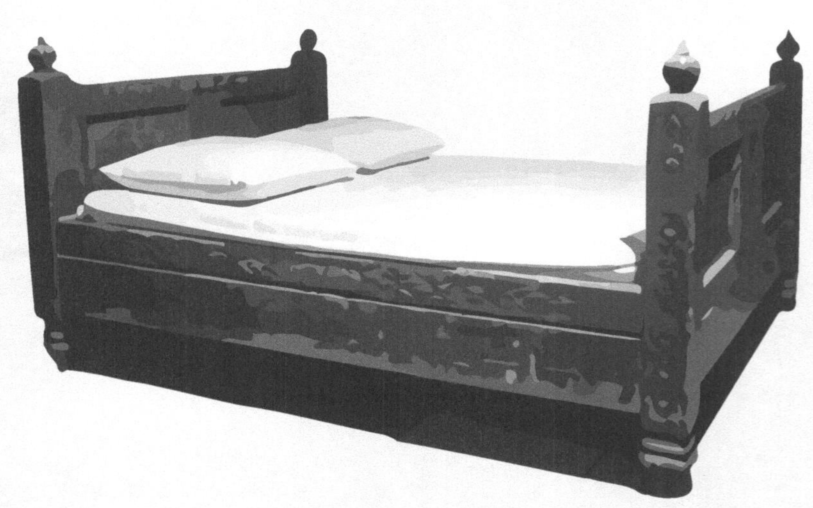

The Precious Vessel

Prophet Yusuf gave the brothers plenty of food. This time they received even more because Binyamin was with them. The wise Yusuf arranged for Binyamin to remain with him. Before the brothers' departure, Yusuf's assistants, on his orders, quietly placed a valuable vessel, the royal measuring cup, in Binyamin's belongings. It was a very expensive vessel, decorated with precious stones. This was not a bad act on the part of Prophet Yusuf, since meanness is impossible to come from any prophet! It was Allah who gave Prophet Yusuf the wise decision to keep Binyamin with him. Subsequently, there was a lot of benefits from this act.

When the brothers drove away a little, Prophet Yusuf sent his people after them. They caught up with the caravan and announced to everyone that the precious vessel of the king had disappeared, and whoever found it or pointed out the thief was promised a reward—he would be given as much more food as the camel could carry. Yusuf's brothers denied that any of them had done this, and swore by Allah that there was no thief among them, and they did not come to Egypt to spread evil. In response to this, one of the assistants asked them, "Then tell me, what punishment is

due to the one with whom we find the missing vessel?" They answered, "The punishment will be the same as is customary with us—the owner will keep the person with whom his thing was found."

Then Yusuf's assistants began to inspect everyone's belongings. So that the brothers would not suspect anything, they started with the eldest brother and so in order they reached the youngest, Binyamin, and pulled out the precious vessel from his bag. Then they took Binyamin to Yusuf.

Yusuf's brothers realized that Binyamin would now be prevented from leaving Egypt and they were powerless to stop it. But they gave their father their word that they would protect Binyamin and return home with him. So, they turned to Yusuf, "Oh, honorable vizier! He has an elderly father who loves him very much and is attached to him. Take pity on his father—let Binyamin go, and take any of us instead. Verily, we see that you are generous and pious." However, Yusuf refused.

When the brothers lost hope of freeing Binyamin, they stepped aside and began to consult what to say to their father. The eldest of them said, "Remember that you promised your father to protect Binyamin and return with him! You once lost Yusuf and did not keep your promise to take care of him, and now you want to return without Binyamin?! I'll stay here and try to free Binyamin! I will not leave Egypt until I receive permission from my father to return. And you go home and tell him everything that happened."

The Grief of Prophet Ya'qub ﷺ

Yusuf's brothers returned to their homeland in Palestine in deep sadness, because they could not keep their promise to their father. They told Prophet Ya'qub what had happened and that the elder brother remained in Egypt, hoping to somehow free him. However, Prophet Ya'qub sensed something was wrong and did not believe that Binyamin could have stolen something. After listening to them, he said, "I don't know what really happened, but you are hiding something from me. Indeed, Allah knows what you do. I will endure and hope that Allah will return all my sons to me."

Prophet Ya'qub felt deep sadness and grief over the loss of two more of his children. This new grief stirred up old feelings in him, pain for his dear son Yusuf. Prophet Ya'qub did not forget about him, although about forty years have passed since then. He began to cry, saying, "What grief and sadness befell me when I lost Yusuf!" Prophet Ya'qub cried so much that he lost his sight.

Then Prophet Ya'qub told his children, "Go back to Egypt and try to find out something about Yusuf and Binyamin!"

Prophet Yusuf ﷺ Reveals his Secret

Fulfilling their father's request, the brothers again went to Egypt and headed to Yusuf's palace. When entering, they said, hoping for his mercy and kindness, "Oh, vizier! We have been hit by a severe drought and our people are in a very difficult situation due to hunger. We came to buy food but the goods we brought with us for payment are not very good. But since we have nothing else, we hope that you will be generous and take these items in exchange for food." They also asked Yusuf to be supportive and return Binyamin to them.

Yusuf felt pity for them, and tears flowed from his eyes. He could no longer hide the truth and said, "What a great evil you committed when you threw Yusuf in the bottom of the well! You cruelly separated him from his brother, as well as from his father and mother, and you don't even realize how much suffering you caused them!"

Then the brothers realized that Yusuf was in front of them. Amazed, they exclaimed, "Truly, you are Yusuf!" Prophet Yusuf said, "Yes, it's me - Yusuf! And this is my brother. Allah has given us special benefits. Truly, whoever shows piety and endures difficulties sincerely for the sake of Allah, Allah will grant him a great reward!"

Hearing this, the brothers realized what superiority Yusuf had over them, and what a high degree Allah had granted him! They also admitted that they had acted very badly and caused a lot of suffering to their families. They stood in front of their brother Yusuf, a high dignitary who was in charge of the treasury and food supplies, and waited to see what he would do with them now.

However, Prophet Yusuf was merciful and had a great character. He did not take revenge or punish them. He forgave his brothers and told them: "I have forgiven you and will not reproach you for the past."

The Blessed Shirt of Prophet Yusuf 

After Prophet Yusuf revealed himself to his brothers, he asked them about their father. Prophet Yusuf missed him greatly. The brothers replied that their father was very weak and that he became blind because he cried a lot, worrying about him. He felt sorry for his father and asked his brothers to give Ya'qub his own shirt. He told them: "Go with my shirt to your father and put it on his face; his vision will return. Then return to me in this country with your father, mother and your families."

Prophet Yusuf's shirt contained blessing (barakah) because it had touched his blessed body. One of the brothers said, "I will take this shirt and go with it to my father. After all, it was I who then brought him a shirt stained with blood, and told him the sad news that Yusuf was eaten by a wolf. Now I want to make him happy that Yusuf is alive!"

The caravan in which Yusuf's brothers were returning home left Egypt and headed to Palestine, to the region of Canaan. With this caravan, Yusuf also sent his father two hundred camels loaded with food. Prophet Ya'qub was waiting for them, hoping for good news. At this time, by the Will of Allah Almighty, a pleasant wind blew, bringing relief to those who were suffering. This wind brought the smell of Yusuf's shirt to Prophet Ya'qub, although there was a huge distance between them! Prophet Ya'qub said to his grandchildren and those around him, "Truly, I smell the scent of my beloved Yusuf!

Having reached home, Yusuf's brother, who was carrying his shirt, immediately went to his father to tell him the good news. He said that Yusuf was alive and gave him his shirt, and that he was waiting for them all to come to him in Egypt. Then he covered Ya'qub's face with Yusuf's blessed shirt, and by the Will of Allah Almighty, Ya'qub's sight returned—he began to see again, as before!

After this, the sons of Prophet Ya'qub turned to their father, "Oh, our father! Ask Allah for forgiveness for us. Verily, we admit that we were sinners." Prophet Ya'qub promised that he would make supplication for them.

The Long-awaited Meeting

Having received news from Yusuf, Prophet Ya'qub and his entire family (around 63 of them) went to Egypt. As they were approaching the city, Prophet Yusuf asked permission from the king to meet his relatives at the city's entrance gate. The King allowed him and even ordered his assistants to go with him to meet the honored guests. So Prophet Yusuf went to meet his loved ones, accompanied by 4,000 soldiers, and ordinary people also came with him.

After meeting his parents, Prophet Yusuf addressed all his relatives with the words, "Welcome to Egypt. Live here in peace and safety!" and invited them to his palace.

In the palace, Prophet Yusuf showed special respect to his parents and seated them on his throne next to him. After this, Yusuf's father, mother and eleven brothers prostrated to him as a greeting—as a sign of respect, and not as worship. This was permitted in the Shari'ah of that time and remained allowed until it was abolished in the Shari'ah of Prophet Muhammad. In our time it is forbidden to bow to the ground to a person, even as a greeting.

After this, Prophet Yusuf said to Prophet Ya'qub: "O father! My dream of the sun, moon, and eleven stars prostrating to me, which I had a long time ago, has come true!" Then Prophet Yusuf continued: "Allah has given me a great blessing; He has given me freedom from captivity after severe trials and suffering, and also given me a high position and the power to dispose of the wealth of all Egypt. Also, by the Will of Allah and His Power, you came to me, to Egypt, after the devil turned my brothers against me. Truly, Allah knows everything, and nothing is hidden from Him!" After this, Prophet Yusuf praised Allah for the blessings he bestowed on him.

Death of Prophet Yusuf ﷺ

Prophet Yusuf ﷺ lived 110 years. After his death, he requested that his body be transferred from Egypt to Palestine, where his ancestors were buried. Four hundred years later, Prophet Moses ﷺ, fulfilled the will of Prophet Yusuf ﷺ and reburied him in Palestine.

The story of Prophet Yusuf is a fascinating one filled with lessons about faith, patience, forgiveness, honesty, chastity, and trust in Allah. His life is a powerful example of how these virtues can lead to success and ultimate triumph despite challenges and hardships.

PROPHET AYYUB (JACOB) 

Lineage of Prophet Ayyub

Prophet Ayyub was a descendant of Ishaq, the son of Prophet Ibrahim.

Known for his piety and gratitude, Ayyub faced many hardships but always remained obedient to Allah, showing immense patience in difficult times and trust in the Almighty.

Patience of Prophet Ayyub 

Prophet Ayyub lived in Al-Bathaniyyah, a village he owned in Hawran, located between Damascus and Jordan. He was blessed with good health, many children, and plenty of fertile lands and livestock. Despite his wealth, he stayed humble, always praising Allah. He was compassionate towards the poor, visiting them and treating them with kindness. He helped the widows and orphans, and he was generous to guests.

Prophets are the best of Allah's creations. They never commit major sins or vile acts. Allah afflicts them with many hardships to elevate their rank in Paradise. Prophet Muhammad said, "Those who are afflicted with the most trials are the prophets; then the more pious a person is, the more trials they face."

For many years, Prophet Ayyub and his family lived in

happiness and prosperity. Then, a series of calamities struck Prophet Ayyub, and he lost all his wealth, including his livestock, fields, and property. Despite his devastating losses, he continued to trust in Allah's wisdom, and remained patient. He said, "Allah owns what He gives me and what He takes from me. He is the Lord of everything! Praise be to Allah Almighty, no matter what happens!"

The troubles of Prophet Ayyub ﷺ didn't stop there. His house was destroyed, and all his children died under the rubble. Prophet Ayyub ﷺ grieved, but his faith remained strong.

Then, Prophet Ayyub ﷺ became seriously ill for 18 years! Yet, he continued to worship Allah, praising Him day and night.

Ayyub's illness was not repulsive or disgusting; his body did not rot and worms did not come out of it. Allah protected His prophets from anything that would turn people away from listening to their message. They were the best and most attractive of people.

Rahma, Prophet Ayyub's wife ﷺ, was the daughter of Prophet Yusuf ﷺ. She was pious, beautiful, and loyal. Despite all the hardships, she stayed by Ayyub's side ﷺ, caring for him and remembering how well he treated her when they lived in prosperity. She did this for the sake of Allah, hoping for reward on the Day of Judgment.

Healing of Prophet Ayyub ﷺ

When Prophet Ayyub ﷺ became poor and sick, most people abandoned him. Only two believers continued to visit him regularly, but one of them eventually stopped coming. When Ayyub asked about him, he learned that this man lost his Faith. The devil had deceived him by saying that Allah doesn't test prophets and pious, so he stopped believing Ayyub was a prophet. This deeply upset Prophet Ayyub ﷺ, who then worried others might do the same. So, he prayed to Allah for healing.

Allah answered his prayer and miraculously healed Prophet Ayyub ﷺ. One day, when Ayyub left his house, Allah commanded him to strike the ground. Two springs appeared. Prophet Ayyub ﷺ drank from one, and all his ailments disappeared. When he washed his body with water from the second spring, he became more handsome and younger than before! Then, two pieces of white cloth were lowered from heaven: one to wrap around the lower part of his body and the other to drape over his shoulders.

Rahma, waiting for her husband, became worried about his long absence. When Prophet Ayyub ﷺ returned healthy and strong, she didn't recognize him. She saw a young, handsome man approaching and asked, "May Allah bless you! Have you met my husband, Ayyub, who has had many trials? I swear by Allah, I've never met a person more like him before his illness than you!" Ayyub ﷺ answered her: "Truly, I am Ayyub!"

Relief after Difficulties

Allah restored the youth and beauty of Prophet Ayyub ﷺ and his wife. After his healing, Rahma bore him 27 sons. Some scholars say Allah resurrected his 14 deceased children and Rahma gave birth to 14 more.

Allah also gave back to Prophet Ayyub his wealth. Ayyub ﷺ had two threshing floors: one for wheat and one for barley. By Allah's Will, two clouds appeared above them. From the cloud above the wheat floor, gold rained down, filling it completely. Another cloud rained silver over the barley floor. Additionally, Allah sent a cloud to where Prophet Ayyub's house had been, which rained golden locusts for three days and nights.

The Great Example of Prophet Ayyub ﷺ

Allah granted Prophet Ayyub all these miracles as a reward for his patience and to honor him ﷺ. He lived for many more years, obeying Allah's commands and calling people to Islam. Despite his wealth, he didn't let it consume him; instead he used it to help the Muslim community. Prophet Ayyub passed away at the age of 93.

The story of Prophet Ayyub ﷺ teaches us to always trust in Allah and to be patient during difficult times. His patience is a shining example for all believers. Today, when people talk about patience, they often remember the great patience of Prophet Ayyub ﷺ and feel inspired to stay strong through their own trials.

Important Note: A Devil Cannot Control A Prophet

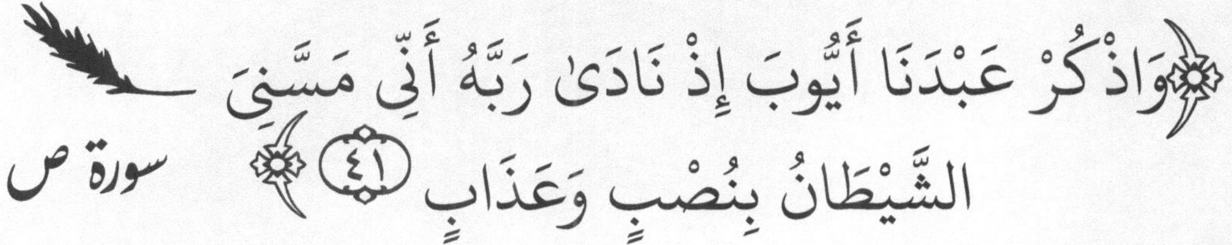

Which means: "And remember our slave Ayyub, when he called to His Lord, 'Indeed, Satan has touched me with hardship and torment'".

In this verse, it is mentioned that the devil affected Prophet Ayyub with hardships. This refers to the story of a few people who used to visit Ayyub during his illness. One of them stopped visiting because he was misguided by the devil and apostatized due to the devil's whisperings about Prophet Ayyub. Prophet Ayyub became saddened by this incident and asked Allah to cure him, so no one else leaves Islam because of his illness. This is supported by the verses that followed, where Allah answered his supplication and granted him miraculous healing through the two springs of water:

﴿وَاذْكُرْ عَبْدَنَا أَيُّوبَ إِذْ نَادَى رَبَّهُ أَنِّي مَسَّنِيَ
الشَّيْطَانُ بِنُصْبٍ وَعَذَابٍ ﴿٤١﴾ ارْكُضْ بِرِجْلِكَ هَذَا
مُغْتَسَلٌ بَارِدٌ وَشَرَابٌ ﴿٤٢﴾ وَوَهَبْنَا لَهُ أَهْلَهُ وَمِثْلَهُم
مَعَهُمْ رَحْمَةً مِّنَّا وَذِكْرَى لِأُولِي الْأَلْبَابِ ﴿٤٣﴾﴾

سورة ص

Which means: "Strike with your foot, this is a spring for a cool bath and drink. And We restored his family to him, and the like thereof with them, as a mercy from Us and a reminder for those of understanding."

It is important to note here that the devil cannot drown the prophets in sins and have no control over them as mentioned in this verse of the Qur'an:

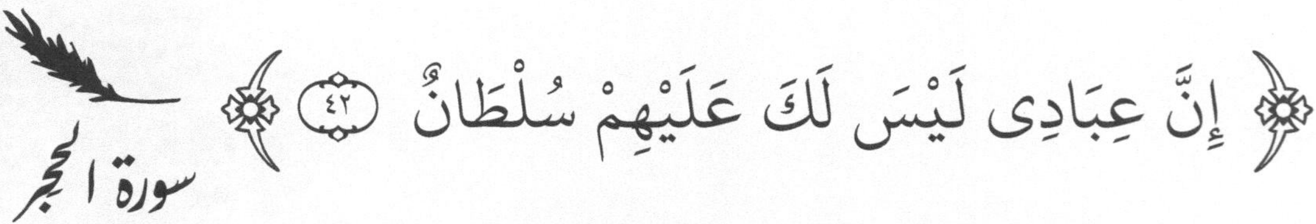

A devil cannot speak through the tongue of any prophet, cannot possess a prophet, and cannot affect him in his mind.

DHUL-KIFL ﷺ

Dhul-kifl, whose original name was Bishr, was the son of Prophet Ayyub ﷺ. He was known as Dhul-Kifl, a title given to him because he took on the responsibility of caring for his people, managing their affairs, and ensuring justice among them. Although we don't have many details about his life or miracles, what we do know is that, like all prophets, he called people to worship Allah alone and lived a life of unwavering faith. The prophets themselves remain faithful all their life and never blasphemed—left Islam—not even for a moment. We also know that they were all endowed with the best human qualities and devoid of all bad qualities. All of them were chosen by God and are the best of His creations. All prophets had beautiful faces and voices and spoke eloquently. They were all attributed with truthfulness, justice, honesty, courage, intelligence, and great manners. It is impossible for them to be attributed with foolishness or vileness. Vileness describes behaviors that are despicable, dishonorable, or degrading that denotes a low character (baseness). Prophets never steal or lie; rather, prophets have the highest moral character.

It is believed that Dhul-Kifl lived until the age of 75 and that he was buried in the area of Nablus in Palestine, a region rich in prophetic history. Many Prophets indeed lived and taught in the Levant (Bilad ash-Sham). Palestine, with Jerusalem (Al-Quds) in particular, often referred to as "Umm Bilad ash-Sham", holds a special place as the heart of this blessed land, making it a pivotal area in the stories of many prophets.

PROPHET YŪNUS (JONAS) 

People of Prophet Yunus

Yunus, the son of Matta, was a descendant of Prophet Ya'qub through his son Binyamin. Allah commanded him to call the inhabitants of Nineveh (Ninwah), a city in the land of Mosul in northern Iraq, to Islam. The people there were idol worshipers; their main idol was called 'Ashtar. It is believed that the population of Nineveh was more than 100,000.

Fulfilling the command of Allah, Prophet Yunus went to Nineveh to call its people to monotheism. Despite his efforts, they rejected his call and continued to worship their idols.

Prophet Yunus ﷺ displayed great patience and called them to Islam for 33 years, using different methods in the hope they would listen. He warned them about the consequences of disbelief and the rewards for those who believe, but their hearts remained hard, and they did not accept the truth.

Throughout this period, only two people believed in him. Eventually, Prophet Yunus ﷺ lost hope that his people would change and left them, but his mistake was leaving before Allah's permission was given to leave them.

Repentance of the inhabitants of Nineveh

Before leaving the city, Prophet Yunus ﷺ warned its inhabitants that they would face punishment in three days if they did not believe. The next morning, black clouds began to gather, and thick smoke appeared over the city blocking the sunlight. The people realized that the punishment Prophet Yunus ﷺ had warned them about was near. Filled with fear, they regretted not heeding his call and sought to repent.

They sought out an elderly, wise man in the community who advised them to repent sincerely and believe in Allah. The people immediately repented and turned to Allah, asking for His forgiveness. Everyone in the city cried out to Allah for mercy. They put on coarse woolen clothing and sprinkled ashes on their heads and started praying to Allah to forgive them. With a loud voice and with humility in their hearts, they cried out to Allah, asking for mercy and salvation. Everyone cried: men, women, children, and even their cattle and riding animals roared loudly. Their repentance from disbelief by embracing Islam was sincere. So Allah forgave them and lifted the punishment.

Prophet Yunus's Trial ﷺ

Unaware of his people's repentance, Prophet Yunus ﷺ had already left Nineveh. He journeyed to the sea, where he boarded a ship. As the ship sailed far out to sea, a violent storm arose and huge waves crashed on the ship. Gripped with intense fear of drowning, the crew believed that someone on board was the cause of the trouble. They decided to draw lots to determine who should be cast overboard to appease the storm. Each time they drew lots, the result pointed to Prophet Yunus. However, since everyone saw him as a pious man, they did not dare to throw him into the sea.

Recognizing that this was a test from Allah, Prophet Yunus willingly left the ship and jumped into the sea, confident that Allah would protect him. Yunus jumped into the depths of the sea because he was sure that Allah would save him, and he would not drown, and there would be no harm to him, not to commit suicide!

Allah grants the prophets amazing miracles! It is impossible for any prophet to kill anyone unjustly or to commit suicide. These are big sins that all prophets are protected from.

Allah commanded a great whale to swallow Yunus without causing him any harm, and it then plunged into the depths of the sea. While Inside the belly of the whale, Prophet Yunus ﷺ was surrounded by three darknesses— the darkness of the night, the darkness of the sea and the darkness inside the fish. Amidst this, Prophet Yunus ﷺ heard the praises of the sea creatures glorifying Allah. Realizing the gravity of his situation, he prayed a special supplication, asking for Allah's forgiveness and praising

Allah Almighty:

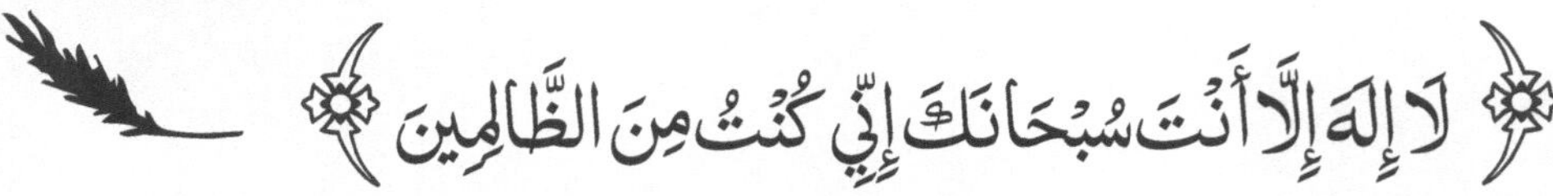

which means, "There is no God except You; exalted are You. Indeed, I have been of the wrongdoers.

Yunus acknowledged his mistake in leaving his people without Allah's permission and repented from this small sin.

Allah accepted his prayer and commanded the whale to release Prophet Yunus onto the shore, unharmed. Yunus spent three days inside the belly of the whale. Yunus, even in the belly of a whale, was grateful to his Creator – he said dhikr, trusting in His Mercy.

The Miraculous Salvation of Prophet Yunus 

After being released by the whale, Prophet Yunus found himself on a desolate shore near the city of Sidon, along the Mediterranean coast, south of present-day Lebanon. He was physically exhausted and had no shelter. By Allah's mercy, a pumpkin tree grew nearby, providing him with shade and nourishment. The tree's large, soft leaves protected him from the sun and insects, while the fruit helped restore his strength.

Allah further provided for Prophet Yunus ﷺ by sending a wild goat to feed him with its milk every morning and evening. All this is by the Mercy of Allah, who granted salvation and safety to Prophet Yunus ﷺ in this difficult situation.

Return of Prophet Yunus ﷺ

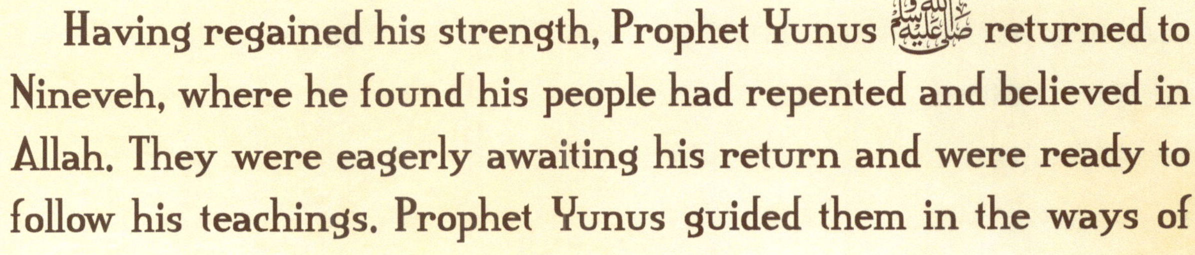

Having regained his strength, Prophet Yunus ﷺ returned to Nineveh, where he found his people had repented and believed in Allah. They were eagerly awaiting his return and were ready to follow his teachings. Prophet Yunus guided them in the ways of

Islam, teaching them the laws of Shari'ah and how to live according to Allah's commands.

A Verse from Al-Qur'an about Prophet Yunus

In the Qur'an, Prophet Yunus is referred to as "Dhu'n-Nun" (the man of the whale). Noon in Arabic means "big fish". Allah said in Chapter of Al-Anbiya' verse 87:

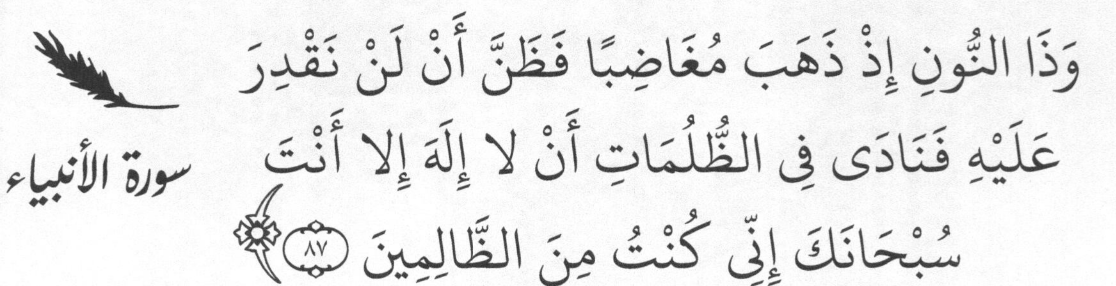

Which means: "And [mention] Dhul-Noon, when he went off displeased at the people not accepting Islam and thought that We would not decree constraint or hardship on him. And he called out within the darknesses, "There is no God except You; exalted are You. Indeed, I have been of the wrongdoers."

This verse highlights that Prophet Yunus left his people out of frustration with their disbelief, angry with them, not out of anger with Allah. It also emphasizes that Prophet Yunus, like all prophets, believed firmly in Allah's power over everything. The word "qadara" in Arabic has multiple meanings—it can refer to power or making a situation difficult. In this context, it means that Prophet Yunus thought Allah would not make his situation difficult for leaving his people prematurely.

PROPHET MŪSĀ (MOSES) 

Background and Birth

Musa is the third best prophet ever. Musa was born in a period of intense strife and oppression in Egypt. The Pharaoh of the time, was not just a tyrant; he proclaimed himself a god, demanding worship from his subjects. He enforced brutal policies, particularly against the Muslim Israelites, including enslavement and genocide.

One day, Pharaoh had a dream that a flame arose in the lands of Jerusalem and came to Egypt. This fire burned the houses, leaving only the homes of Ya'qub's descendants. He was very frightened and called his soothsayers. They interpreted his dream that a child will be born among the Israelites and would grow up to overthrow him. Terrified for his rule, Pharoah ordered the massacre of all newborn Israelite boys.

After some time, out of fear that in the future there would be no one to do all the hard work, the pharaoh's entourage asked him to relax this decree. Pharaoh agreed and ordered that newborn boys be killed every other year.

Birth of Musa

Musa's mother, Yuhanidh, was a remarkable woman of strong faith. She got pregnant with Moses during the year when Pharaoh's forces were ruthlessly killing the male infants of the Children of Israel. Despite the danger, she managed to conceal her pregnancy, trusting in Allah.

Allah granted her to know that her child was destined for a great future and that Pharaoh's attempts to destroy him would fail.

When Musa was born, Yuhanidth cared for her son with immense love and tenderness. To protect him from Pharoah's soldiers, she devised a plan. She placed Musa in a small basket, lined it with soft bedding, and tied it securely to the bank of the Nile River, which flowed near their home. Whenever Pharoah's soldiers searched the houses of the Israelites for newborn boys, she would hide Musa in the basket.

One day, however, Yuhanidth forgot to tie the basket to the riverbank. The current carried it away, and the basket floated along the Nile's waves. Allah guided the basket to the

very place of Pharaoh's. It landed on the shore near the royal residence, where Pharaoh's wife's maids discovered it. Initially, they assumed it contained something valuable and brought it to Asiyah, Pharaoh's wife.

Asiyah[1], known for her compassion and wisdom, opened the basket and saw the infant inside. She was immediately captivated by his innocence and beauty. Despite the cruelty of her husband, she felt an overwhelming attachment to the child and resolved to protect him. This moment marked the beginning of an extraordinary journey, one that would change the course of history.

1 Asiyah the daughter of Muzahim, was a pious woman. In fact, she is the fourth best woman in rank after Lady Maryam, Lady Fatimah, and Lady Khadijah. Allāh mentioned her and Lady Maryam in the Qur'an as an example for the believers. According to the Shari'ah of that time, a Muslim woman was allowed to be married to an unbeliever. Asiyah initially concealed her faith from her husband, fearing that he might kill her. However, when she openly stood against his oppression and declared her belief, Pharaoh discovered her faith. He then tortured her severely, leading to her martyrdom.

The Story of Musa's Feeding

After Asiyah opened the basket and saw the beautiful baby there with light between his eyes, she decided to raise him herself, since she did not have children with Pharoah. The cruel pharaoh did not share this joy with her and ordered the boy to be killed. However, Asiyah was able to convince Pharaoh to keep the child.

The news that a boy was found in a basket that appeared in the palace quickly spread among the people. Musa's mother immediately realized that this was her son. She was grieving and did not know what to do next, greatly missing her child. She asked her daughter Maryam, Musa's sister, to go to the palace and find out how things were going there. Without wasting time, Maryam went there and saw baby Musa crying from hunger because he did not drink the milk of any woman who was brought to him.

Quietly approaching Asiyah, Musa's sister said that she knew a reliable and honest woman who could be a wet-nurse for the child and care for him for a certain fee. This is how Prophet Musa's mother ended up in the palace. Seeing her child, Musa's mother was happy, the baby enjoyed the milk to his fill and fell asleep.

Asiyah was very pleased and invited this woman to live in their palace and promised a generous reward for her help in this. Musa's mother explained that she could not afford this, because there were other children waiting for her at home, whom she could not leave. She asked Asiyah for permission to take the child to her home. Asiyah had no choice but to agree, but she asked her to bring Musa to her from time to time so that she could see him grow. She also undertook to provide him with everything he needed. So, by the Will of Allah, Musa returned to his mother safe and sound. Allah protected him from reprisals in the palace of the man who most wanted his death—in the palace of the evil pharaoh.

Growing Up in the Palace

Musa, known for his striking appearance and sharp intellect, was raised in Pharoah's palace. Loved dearly by Asiyah, and eventually earning a place in Pharoah's heart, Musa blossomed into a charismatic young man.

A Fateful Encounter

One day, Pharoah went on a trip, and Musa followed but stopped to rest in a city in old Egypt. It was during the hottest part of the day, the streets nearly empty as people sheltered from the sun. That's when he stumbled upon a fight—a Muslim from the Children of Israel being assaulted by a Copt, one of the followers of Pharoah. The Israelite called Musa to help save him. Musa approached the Copt, wanting to stop the injustice. He wanted to push this man away and he hit him with his hand. Though Musa did not intend to kill this person, the Copt fell dead. Musa was very strong. Prophets are the strongest people. Musa began to regret what he had done. A prophet must not fight his enemies until he receives the permission to do so. This was a small non-demeaning sin from Musa. Musa repented and Allah accepted his repentance.

While in the city, Moses feared that he would be harmed when they found out that he had killed that man in defense of his fellow tribesman, and they would realize who he was and this would lead to serious consequences. No one except that Israelite saw how the unbelieving Copt died at the hands of Moses. Pharaoh's followers reported what had happened to him and he was very angry that an Israelite had killed one of them. Meanwhile, while they were looking for the killer, Moses again happened to pass by that same Israelite he defended the previous day. He was fighting with another Copt and called Moses for help. Moses came closer and wanted to stop the follower of Pharaoh, but it seemed to the Israelite that he swung at him so he said: "Oh, Moses, do you really want to kill me, just like you killed that man yesterday?!" The Copt, hearing these words, left him and hurried to Pharaoh to notify him of this. Pharaoh ordered that Moses be found and killed so that none of the Israelites would dare to kill any of Pharaoh's followers.

A New Beginning in Madyan

The soldiers went in search of Musa through the streets of the city. But one believer from the family of Pharaoh named Hizkeel who was hiding his belief, learned about the conspiracy against Moses. He hurried to Moses and told him that they wanted to kill him and advised him to leave the city.

Musa left Egypt on foot without provisions. After eight days of travel, Musa arrived in Madyan exhausted. He stopped to rest near a well. There he encountered two young women struggling to water their flocks amidst a crowd of shepherds. The two young women were trying not to let their animals mix with the flock of other shepherds. Musa asked about their situation to which they replied that there are no sons in their family, and their father is very old, so they have to help with the housework and do difficult work outside too. Returning home, these girls rushed to tell their father Prophet Shu'ayb, that they had met a young man who helped them. Shu'ayb, to return this act of kindness, asked one of his daughters to invite him over.

Welcomed warmly and treated to a meal, Musa shared his story with Shu'ayb, who reassured him of his safety from Pharoah's reach in Madyan. Impressed by Musa's character, Shu'ayb offered his daughter's hand in marriage, under the condition that Musa would work for him for eight years. Grateful and seeking stability, Musa agreed, eventually choosing to extend his stay two more years out of his noble character and gratitude to the family.

Return to Egypt

Years later, a longing for his homeland and family prompted Musa to return to Egypt with his own family. By that time, Musa already had two sons, and his wife was pregnant with her third child. And so, Musa, taking his family, provisions, and a flock of sheep, set off on the road back to Egypt.

Along the way, they faced harsh conditions and became lost. During a particularly cold night, unable to light a fire, Musa noticed a distant glow on Mount Ṯur. He headed there to try to get his family some fire to warm themselves with.

There, Musa received Revelation from Allah. Allah gave Musa the ability to hear His eternal Kalam which is not a speech made of letters or sound. The Kalam of Allah is not in any language, neither Arabic nor Hebrew. All languages are created. The Kalam of Allah is an attribute of Allah that is not created; rather, the Kalam of Allah has no beginning and no end.

Musa understood from this eternal Kalam that Allah is ordering him to take off his shoes because he was in the blessed valley of Ṯuba. Allah informed Musa that he has been chosen and ordered him to listen to the Revelation that he receives.

Allah revealed to Musa to throw his staff on the ground. By the Will of Allah, the staff turned into a huge, fast-moving snake! It was so big and intimidating that Musa, without looking back, hurried to move away from it. Prophet Musa ﷺ, like all Prophets, was very brave, but the transformation of his staff into a huge snake was unexpected for him. Allah revealed to Musa not to be afraid. When Musa returned, Allah ordered him to pick up the snake. As soon as Musa took hold of the snake, it turned back into a staff. Also, Allah commanded Prophet Musa ﷺ to put his hand in the opening of his garment. And when Musa took it out, his hand glowed with an amazing white light.

Allah's Command to Musa and Harun to Call Pharaoh to Islam

Equipped with miracles and accompanied by his brother Harun (Aaron), Prophet Musa ﷺ set out on his mission to call Pharaoh and his followers to monotheism. Prophet Musa ﷺ also asked Allah to grant him support, to ease his case, strengthen his heart, and to grant ease to his tongue when talking, so that Pharaoh and his followers would not reject him and harm him and his brother Prophet Harun ﷺ.

Prophet Musa was eloquent, his speech was clear and wise. But Musa ﷺ asked Allah for relief from a minor difficulty in his tongue from the trace of a coal that burned his tongue when he was a baby.

The Meeting of Prophet Musa and Pharaoh

Musa and his brother came to the grand palace of the pharaoh. When the guards asked them what they wanted, Musa ﷺ replied, "Tell Pharaoh that the Messenger of the Lord of the Worlds is at the gate." With great courage, they stood before Pharaoh and his court, steadfastly delivering their message. Musa called Pharoah to believe in Allah and demanded that he stop oppressing the people of Israel and set them free.

Pharaoh was astonished at the courage of these two men, especially when he recognized one of them. "Aren't you the same Musa whom we raised in this palace? And aren't you the one who committed that deed?" Pharoah was referring to the incident where Musa, by mistake, had killed a Copt.

Pharaoh, refusing to acknowledge Allah, argued with Musa, claiming to be the only god. When Pharoah found himself with no more arguments, he resorted to threats, warning Musa of imprisonment.

Musa and the Sorcerers

Pharoah, seeing that Musa and Harun were not intimidated, continued to threaten them. Musa responded, "What if I show irrefutable proof?" He threw his staff on the ground, and it instantly turned into a massive, living snake! Pharaoh was terrified. Musa then placed his hand into the opening of his garment, and when he removed it, his hand shone with a brilliant white light. When he repeated the movement, his hand returned to normal.

Pharaoh, desperate to discredit Musa, accused him of performing sorcery (as-sihr) and demanded a challenge. Musa agreed to meet Pharoah's sorcerers at an appointed time and place. Pharaoh gathered the most skilled sorcerers from across the kingdom, promising them great rewards if they could defeat Musa.

Sorcery (السِحْر) is a forbidden act, a big sin, as it involves the help of devils, our enemies. During Pharaoh's time, magic was widespread, and those who performed the most unusual tricks were considered powerful.

On the appointed day, a large crowd gathered to witness the contest. Pharoah's sorcerers, feeling confident in their abilities, asked Musa, "Will you begin, or shall we?" Musa did not prompt the sorcerers to commit an enormous sin. Rather, he spoke to them in a rebuking manner. Pharaoh and his court watched eagerly. The sorcerers threw their ropes and staffs, which appeared to transform into slithering snakes, tricking the eyes of the onlookers.

But when Musa threw his staff, it turned into a real, enormous snake that devoured the sorcerer's illusions, all those ropes and staffs that had seemed like snakes. The sorcerers, realizing that this was no ordinary magic but a true miracle from Allah, were astonished. Well versed in the tricks of sorcery, they immediately recognized the truth: what Prophet Musa had demonstrated was not sorcery, and no magic could oppose. Overwhelmed with the truth, they declared," We believe in the Lord of Harun and Musa."

Pharaoh was enraged. He had never imagined that the very people he intended to use against Musa would turn and support him instead. Furious and humiliated, Pharoah threatened them with severe punishment. Yet, despite Pharoah's threats, they remained steadfast in their new faith, refusing to renounce Islam.

Pharaoh, in his arrogance and cruelty, refused to heed the call of Prophet Musa. He executed the former sorcerers, who died as martyrs and will be granted eternal happiness in Paradise. But for Pharaoh and his followers, great trouble and suffering lay ahead.

The Detailed Signs Sent to Pharaoh's Followers

The first two signs were the transformation of Prophet Musa's staff and the emission of light from his hand. Musa's staff could turn into a huge snake, but it also had other miraculous qualities: it could become like a tree bearing fruit, a lamp emitting light, or even a rope with a bucket at the end. Now, let's explore the remaining signs in more detail.

Prophet Musa warned Pharaoh and his followers that Allah would punish them for their disbelief and rejection of His Messenger. In time, Musa's warning came true. Allah subjected Pharaoh and his people to a series of punishments that lasted for several years. When good times returned, they arrogantly claimed, "This is due to our own efforts." But when calamity struck, they would turn to Musa, asking him to pray to Allah to remove the punishment, promising that they would then believe. However, each time the punishment was lifted, they went back on their word and continued in their disbelief. Some even blamed Musa for bringing these troubles upon them, accusing him of witchcraft. These calamities, often referred to as the plagues of Egypt, were extraordinary phenomena.

The Flood and the Locusts

First, a drought struck Egypt, lasting several years and plunging the land into unbearable heat and dust. Crop failures followed, and trees stopped producing fruit. During the flowering season, gardens appeared normal, but the flowers didn't bear fruit, leaving the trees barren. This led to widespread hunger and devastation. Neither Pharaoh, his army, nor his remaining sorcerers could stop these misfortunes.

Then came the flood, which covered the land with water, demolishing buildings and destroying crops and gardens. Despite living in adjacent homes, water only flooded the houses of the Copts, while the homes of the Israelites remained dry. The flood lasted eight days and nights until the Copts, desperate, begged Musa to pray for relief, promising to believe in Allah. Musa prayed, and the flood receded. The earth dried, and plants began to grow again in abundance. However, once relieved, the Copts broke their promise and refused to believe in Musa.

As punishment, Allah sent hordes of locusts that darkened the sky and covered the earth, eating all crops, fruits, and even household items like clothes, furniture, and doors. Yet, the homes of the Israelites were untouched. The Copts again turned to Musa, promising to repent if the locusts were removed. Musa prayed and pointed his staff towards the east and the west, and the locusts returned to where they

came from, leaving a small amount of crops uneaten. But instead of keeping their promise, the Copts arrogantly declared that what remained was sufficient and refused to accept Islam.

Lice and Frogs

Next, came an invasion of lice. Musa pointed his staff at 'Ayn Shams, a hill in Egypt, and it turned into lice. These tiny insects infested the Copts' animals and crops, invaded their homes, and clung to their skin like bumps from smallpox, causing immense discomfort and depriving them of rest and sleep. The lice even entered their hair, eyelashes, and food. The Copts cried out to Musa, who prayed to Allah, and a hot wind came, burning the lice and throwing them into the sea Yet, the Copts soon returned to their disbelief, accusing Musa of sorcery once more.

The sixth sign was the invasion of frogs, which appeared everywhere—on the streets, in houses, beds, closets, food, and drinks. Frogs even jumped into cooking pots and into the mouths of those trying to speak. Unable to rid themselves of the frogs, the

Copts turned to Musa again, promising to believe. Musa took strong covenants from them, and the frogs died, washed away by rain into the sea. But once more, the Copts broke their promise.

Blood

The seventh and perhaps most difficult sign was when their water turned into blood. The Nile River began flowing with blood. Whenever an Israelite drew water, it remained water, but whenever a Copt drew from it, it turned to blood. Even if a Muslim tried to help a Copt drink, the water would turn into blood in the Copt's mouth. Desperate, Pharaoh himself tried to drink from moist plants, but the sap turned salty in his mouth.

Each of these signs lasted one week, from Saturday to the next Saturday, followed by a month of relief. These signs showed the stubbornness and arrogance of Pharaoh and his followers and established clear evidence against them.

The miracles of Allah are undeniable. When a Prophet shows a miracle, no one, no matter how powerful, can oppose or change it. Pharaoh, who claimed to be a god, was powerless to resist Musa. His anger and frustration grew as each sign proved his claims false and his power to be merely that of a mortal man. In a desperate attempt to hide his weakness, Pharaoh and his advisers decided to exterminate the Israelites, thinking they could erase the evidence of their defeat.

This story reminds us of the consequences of arrogance and stubbornness in the face of truth. Pharaoh and his followers were given multiple chances to recognize the signs of Allah and change their ways, yet they remained defiant and arrogant, leading to their ultimate downfall. This is a powerful lesson in humility and the importance of being open to truth, even when it challenges our pride or preconceived notions.

The story also highlights the dangers of making promises or commitments without sincerity. Pharaoh's followers repeatedly promised to change, only to break their promises once the immediate danger passed. This teaches the value of integrity—keeping your word, especially when it comes to matters of faith and truth.

The Parting of the Sea and Pharaoh's Death

Allah commanded Prophet Musa to lead the Israelites out of Egypt.

One day, 600,000 Muslims, led by Musa and Harun, left Egypt and headed towards Palestine, taking a route that led them to the shores of the Red Sea. Pharaoh, eager to capture and kill them all, saw this as an opportunity. He believed the Israelites had trapped themselves, with the sea in front of them and nowhere to escape. Pharaoh's army, a massive force of more than one and a half million soldiers, including 1,000,000 on horseback, set out in pursuit.

When the Israelites reached the shore of the Red Sea, they feared they were doomed. Pharoah's enormous army was closing in behind them with mountains on both sides and the sea in front of them. It seemed there was no escape. But at Allah's command, Prophet Musa struck the shore with his staff, and a miraculous event occurred–the sea parted, resulting in wide, dry paths between towering walls of water. There were twelve parts or passages, one for each of the twelve tribes of the Israelites, the descendants of the twelve sons of Ya'qub.

Pharaoh and his army arrived at the shore, stunned by the sight before them. They saw the incredible walls of water forming a passageway through the sea and the Israelites approaching the opposite shore. Enraged by the prospect of losing his prey, Pharoah ordered his army to attack. Together they charged into the sea, following the Israelites through the parted water.

Once the last of the Israelites had safely crossed to the other side, and before the first of Pharoah's soldiers could emerge from the sea, Prophet Musa struck the ground with his staff again. The walls of water collapsed, drowning Pharoah and his entire army. Pharoah's body was expelled onto the shore, swollen and lifeless, for all his followers to witness the end of their once-mighty leader.

Pharaoh died as a blasphemer, refusing to believe until the moment he was certain he was about to die, hence, his repentance was not accepted because repentance when one faces imminent death is not accepted. Pharoah is one of the heads of the blasphemers, not only because of his own disbelief, but because he led others to blasphemy and claimed to be a god. His punishment in Hellfire will be far more severe than that of a blasphemer who did not lead others astray.

The miraculous salvation of the people of Israel occurred on the day of 'Ashura', the tenth day of the month of Al-Muharram.

Prophet Musa Receives the Torah

After Allah destroyed Pharaoh, the Israelites asked Prophet Musa to bring them the Scripture that would explain the laws of Allah Almighty. Musa was guided to a specific place where he would receive the revelation.

Musa ﷺ was absent for forty days, during which the sacred Scripture, the Torah, was revealed to him. The Torah was written on tablets in the Hebrew language and contained laws, teachings, and religious matters that the Israelites needed to live according to Allah's guidance.

The Story of Some Israelites Worshipping the Golden Calf

During the forty days of Musa's absence, his brother Harun ﷺ led the people. However, during this time, some troubling events unfolded. An evil man named Samiriyy crafted a figure of a calf from gold, using some soil he had collected from beneath Angel Gabriel when Gabriel was on the Red Sea shore on the day of the great miracle. By the will of Allah, the golden calf began to make a sound, and Samiriyy told the people this was their god that Musa allegedly had forgotten to take with him.

This deception caused a division among the Israelites. Some of them strayed from the true religion and began to worship the golden calf, while others remained steadfast in their belief in Allah. Prophet Harun ﷺ urged the people to abandon the worship of the calf and to adhere to the true religion. However, the misguided ones refused, saying, "We will not stop worshiping him until Musa returns to us."

When Prophet Musa ﷺ returned, he was shocked and angered to see how easily his people had been deceived. He reminded them of the great miracles they witnessed by Allah's Grace and scolded them for straying from the truth in such a short time.

Musa called on them to repent and return to Islam, the true religion.

The Israelites, realizing their grave mistake, blamed Samiriyy for leading them astray.

Musa burned the golden calf and urged those who had departed from the truth to return to monotheism. They repented and returned to Islam. Allah revealed to Prophet Musa the punishment for those who had committed this grave sin, and it was carried out. The name "Yahood" يهود in Arabic is derived from "Hada" (هاد), which means to come back, because the Israelites who had left Islam came back to the true religion. However, many of the Yahood, though, after hundreds of years, left Islam again when they refused to believe in Jesus as a prophet and messenger sent by Allah Almighty.

Prophet Musa ﷺ brought the knowledge contained in the Holy Book of Torah to his people, and warned that those who deviate from Islam will face severe consequences.

The Israelites' Wandering

Prophet Musa ﷺ faced many difficulties and trials with his people, the Israelites. Despite witnessing numerous great miracles, they did not fully obey him. When Musa ordered them to rid the sacred land of Jerusalem from the tyrants who were occupying it, they hesitated and refused. As a punishment for their disobedience, Allah cause them to be lost in a barren wilderness with no water, food, or shade from the scorching sun known as Teeh Bani Isra'eel (التيه), where they wandered for forty years.

Allah provided the Israelites in miraculous ways during this time. He sent clouds to protect them from the sun during the day, and white bread, known as Al-Mann, would descend from the sky like snow. Additionally, winds would bring As-Salwa, or quails, which are birds like pigeons to provide them with meat. Despite these blessings, the Israelites continually asked Musa for more.

Through these challenges, Prophet Musa displayed immense wisdom and patience, fulfilling his prophetic mission. He passed away at the age of 120, and his grave is located very close to the sacred land, near a red sand hill. According to the hadith, Prophet Muhammad visited Musa during the Night Journey of Al-Isra' before entering Jerusalem and found him praying in his grave. It is narrated that all prophets are alive in their graves, praying, as per the hadith of the Prophet:

الأَنبِيَاءُ أَحْيَاءٌ فِي قُبُورِهِم يُصَلُّون

Prophet Musa

Musa died during the period of the Teeh, before the Israelites could enter the sacred land. After the deaths of Musa and Harun, Allah sent Yusha' (Joshua), a young companion of Musa, as a prophet. Yusha' led the Israelites out of the Teeh and into battle against the tyrants in Jerusalem. Yusha' was victorious, and he successfully entered Jerusalem, purifying it from the tyrants. However; none of the people who disobeyed Musa in fighting the tyrants entered the blessed land; they all died in the Teeh prior to that.

PROPHET ILYĀS (ELIJAH) 

Prophet Ilyas ﷺ was a descendant of Harun, ﷺ. He was sent by Allah to guide a nation of idol worshippers back to the true religion of Islam. The ruler of this nation was a tyrant who oppressed the people, and for a time, Prophet Ilyas ﷺ had to hide to escape the ruler's harm. Despite these challenges, Prophet Ilyas continued to call the people to Islam every day for many years.

However, the people stubbornly clung to their ways of ignorance. They only turned to Prophet Ilyas ﷺ during the hardest times, asking for his support, but as soon as they found relief, they quickly forgot and return to their pagan practices. As a result, Prophet Ilyas ﷺ had only a small group of faithful followers.

One day, Prophet Ilyas ﷺ prayed to Allah to punish the idolaters so they might learn a lesson. Allah sent a severe drought that lasted for three long years. During this time, livestock died, trees withered, and the people suffered greatly. Some began to embrace Islam, hoping to end their suffering, and Allah, the Merciful, sent rain to the earth, restoring everything to normal.

Unfortunately, once the drought ended, the people reverted to idolatry, becoming arrogant and cruel once again. When the ruler of the people changed, a new king came to power. Thanks to the call of Prophet Ilyas ﷺ, the new ruler accepted Islam, and many others followed his lead.

Prophet Ilyas ﷺ fulfilled his prophetic mission with dignity.

It is reported that he passed away and was buried in the city of Baalbek, in what is now modern eastern Lebanon.

A lesson to Learn

Have you noticed that one of the severe punishments Allah sent was drought? This shows us that everything happens by the Will of Allah. Not even a single drop of rain falls from the sky unless Allah wills it. Rain brings great benefits to people. So be honest, sincere, and kind, and never forget to thank Allah for all the blessings you have and will have.

PROPHET AL-YASA' (ELISHA) 

Al-Yasa' was a descendent of Prophet Yusuf and a cousin of Prophet Ilyas ﷺ. He lived during the same time as Prophet Ilyas, and became a prophet after his cousin's death, leading the Muslim community.

At that time, the Israelites still possessed a sacred chest known as the Tābūt, which contained relics from Prophet Musa ﷺ and Prophet Harun ﷺ. Whenever they carried this Tābūt into battle, they felt tranquility (sakinah) and emerged victorious. Like his cousin, Prophet Al-Yasa' also faced ignorance, rudeness, and cruelty from the people. Some followed his call, while others rejected it. His name is mentioned in the Holy Qur'an, reminding us of his dedication to spreading truth and justice.

PROPHET DAWŪD 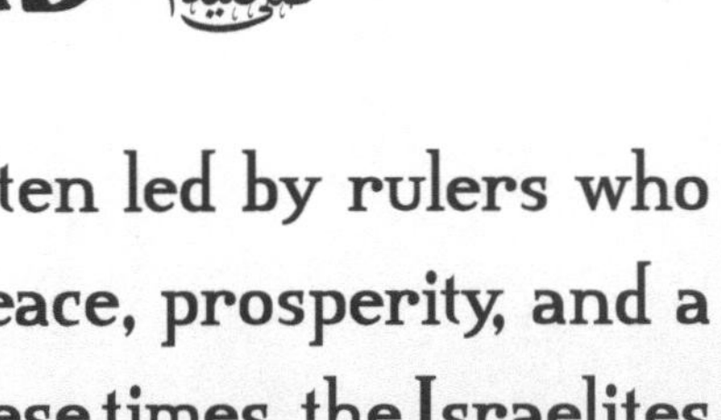

Throughout history, the Israelites were often led by rulers who were also prophets. These leaders brought peace, prosperity, and a sense of righteousness to the people. During these times, the Israelites were devout and followed the teachings of their prophets. However, after a prophet would pass away, the people would often fall back into idolatry and immoral behavior, leading to period of chaos and suffering.

Ṯalūt (Saul) & Jalūt (Goliath)

After the death of Prophets Musa and Harun, Prophet Yusha' (Joshua) became the leader of the Israelites. Under his guidance, they experienced a time of peace and stability. But after Yusha's death, the people once again strayed from the righteous path, turning to idol worship and allowing corruption to spread. This led to a decline in their society, with lawlessness and immorality becoming widespread.

When the Israelites abandoned the teachings of their prophets, Allah would send trials with disaster and oppression from other nations. Often, they faced attacks from surrounding nations. At one point, after the death of a weak ruler, the Israelites found themselves leaderless and vulnerable. Their enemies, including Bedouins Arabs, Armenians, and Philistines, frequently attacked them, stealing their treasures and taking their people as slaves. One such raid resulted in the loss of a sacred chest containing the staff of Prophet Musa.

In their desperation, the Israelites began to long for a strong leader who could unite them and restore their former glory. They remembered the days when they were guided by prophets and righteous kings, and life was just and peaceful. Allah then sent them a Prophet named Shamu'il (Samuel), who called them back to believe in Allah and renounce idolatry. Allah Almighty revealed to Shamu'il that the ruler of the Israelites should be a man named Talut (Saul).

However, the Israelites were not pleased with this choice. Talut was not wealthy nor from a prominent family, and they questioned how he could be their king. They believed that only someone with wealth and status should rule over them. However, Shamu'il reminded them that Allah had chosen Talut for his knowledge and physical strength, and Allah gives power to whomever He wills. The people eventually accepted Talut as their ruler.

Talut soon gathered an army, calling on the strongest men among the Israelites to join him. Despite their desire to end the oppression they faced, only a fraction of the 80,000 men who joined passed the test of obedience set by Allah. Talut had instructed them not to drink

from the Jordan River, except for a sip to quench the thirst, a test of their discipline. Only a small group of just over 300 men resisted the temptation to drink, proving their loyalty.

With this small but devoted army, Talut faced the much larger forces of Jalut (Goliath), a tyrant known for his immense strength and cruelty. Despite their fear and overwhelming odds, the pious among them encouraged their companions to remain steadfast in their faith.

When the battle began, Jalut challenged the Israelites to send forth a warrior to fight him in a single combat (duel). A young man named Dawud (David), who was with his father in Talut's army, stepped forward. Despite his youth. Dawud fearlessly accepted the challenge. Jalut mocked him, but Dawud, armed with only a sling and few small stones, defeated the giant. His victory not only humiliated Jalut but also led to the defeat of the enemy army.

After the battle, Talut gave Dawud his daughter in marriage and gave him half of his wealth and power, marking the beginning of Dawud's journey to becoming a great leader of the Israelites.

The Call of Prophet Dawud ﷺ

Dawud was known for his deep piety, humility, and wisdom as a ruler. When he turned 40, Allah granted him prophethood. Prophet Dawud then began calling the Israelites to adhere to the teachings of the Torah, the Heavenly Book that had been revealed to Prophet Musa. The basis of Dawud's call, like every prophet before and after him, was to believe in Allah, who has absolute power and is unlike His creations.

After some time, Allah revealed the Zaboor to Prophet Dawud. The Zaboor, revealed in the Hebrew language, contained many lessons and guidance for the people. However, it did not introduce new laws or prohibitions, so the Shari'ah (laws) of Prophet Musa continued to be in effect.

The Virtues of Prophet Dawud ﷺ

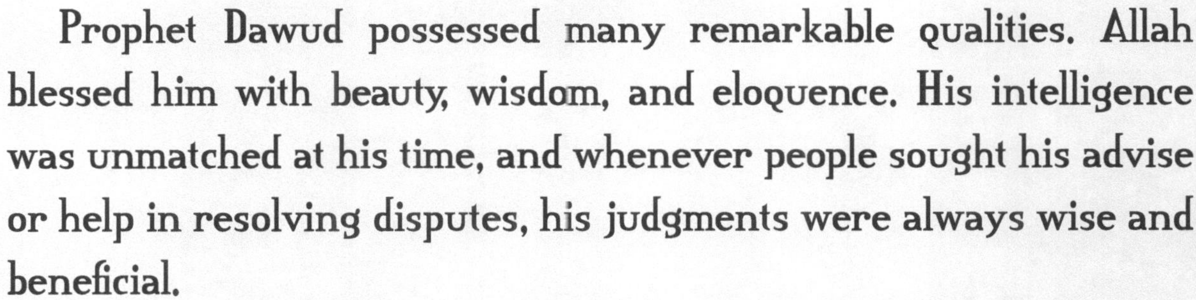

Prophet Dawud possessed many remarkable qualities. Allah blessed him with beauty, wisdom, and eloquence. His intelligence was unmatched at his time, and whenever people sought his advise or help in resolving disputes, his judgments were always wise and beneficial.

One of the most extraordinary gifts Allah bestowed upon Prophet Dawud was his beautiful voice, with which he constantly praised Allah. The mountains, trees, and plants would join in dhikr when he said "SubhanAllah". Even the birds would gather around him,

listening to his praises. This miraculous connection with nature was a sign of Allah's favor upon him.

Despite his power, strength, and wealth, Prophet Dawud was also known for his humility and hardwork. He worked as a blacksmith. Earning his living through his own labor. Prophet Dawud was able to soften iron in his hands as if it were dough, without the need for a hammer, anvil, or fire. He would mold swords and shields with his bare hands, a miraculous ability granted to him by Allah.

Prophet Dawud was also the first to craft iron chain mail, providing his warriors with strong protection in battle. His ingenuity and craftsmanship set a new standard for armor, further showcasing his wisdom and practical skills.

The Story of the Two Brothers' Dispute

Prophet Dawud was both a prophet and a just ruler, known for resolving disputes among his people. One day, while he was in deep worship, two brothers came into his prayer space (mihrab) to seek his judgment. These brothers were business partners in a flock of sheep. One of them said, "My brother owns 99 sheep and I only have one. Now he wants to take my own sheep and add it to his flock."

Hearing this, Prophet Dawud believed the man's claim and immediately judged that the brother with 99 sheep was unjust. Altough Dawud's judgment was correct, he realized that he should have listened to the other brother's side of the story before making a decision. A judge must always hear both sides in any dispute.

Realizing his mistake, Prophet Dawud immediately turned to Allah, asking for forgivness. It's important to know that this small sin was not vile. It was not a demeaning sin.

It is also important here to clear up a common misunderstanding.

Some stories falsely claim that Prophet Dawud sent a commander to war to be killed so that he could marry the man's wife. This is completely untrue and goes against the honorable character of any prophet. The real story, as mentioned in the Qur'an, involves the dispute over the sheep, not anything immoral or deceitful.

Death of Prophet Dawud ﷺ

Prophet Dawud's ﷺ passing was as remarkable as his life. One day, as he returned home, he found a man standing in the middle of his courtyard. Surprised, Prophet Dawud asked, "Who are you?" The person replied, "I am the one who is not afraid of rulers, and no one can keep me out." Dawud immediately recognized him and said, "Then you must be the Angel of Death."

The man was indeed 'Izra'eel, the Angel of Death. After greeting him, Prophet Dawud's soul was taken. Prophet Dawud ﷺ was 100 years old when he passed away leaving behind him a legacy of wisdom, justice, and devotion.

PROPHET SULAYMAN (SOLOMON) ﷺ

Prophet Sulayman was the son of Prophet Dawud ﷺ. Like his father, Sulayman was blessed with immense knowledge, influence, and power. His mother was also a deeply God-fearing woman, who nurtured him with valuable teachings from a young age.

The Power & Kingdom of Sulayman ﷺ

Prophet Sulayman's power was extraordinary—he ruled a vast kingdom that spanned from east to west. Allah granted him a reign that He had not given to anyone else, as mentioned in the Qur'an. He had a thousand houses made of glass, and in his council of judgment, there were 600,000 chairs—some on the right side and some on the left. The believers among humans would sit on some of these chairs, while the jinn (genies) would sit on others. Despite his immense wealth and power, Sulayman's heart was not attached to wordly luxuries. Although he could have indulged in the finest foods—he could have even made bread from milled pearls if he wished—he chose to eat simple barley bread instead of wheat, rice, or corn bread, and his condiment with the barley bread was sour milk. For the people, however, he would slaughter 100,000 sheep every day. He lived and slept modestly, dedicating his strength and resources to spreading the teachings of Islam, worshipping Allah, and ensuring justice and prosperity for his people. Prophet Sulayman was known for his fairness and maintained order in the lands he ruled.

One of the unique blessings given to Prophet Sulayman ﷺ was the ability to command the devils. Even the most powerful among them, like the 'ifrits, were subjugated to him, working under his control and did not dare to disobey him, for they feared the consequences of defiance. Sulayman ﷺ commanded the jinn to build magnificent structures, retrieve treasures from the depths of the sea, and perform tasks that would have been impossible for humans.

By the will of Allah, even the wind was under Sulayman's command!

He possessed a grand majestic platform made of wood, adorned with gold and silk. The wind would lift this platform, allowing Sulayman ﷺ and his entire army, along with their equipment, to travel vast distances in a short time.

In addition to his dominion over the jinn and the elements, Prophet Sulayman was granted the ability to speak the languages of different nations. When addressing these nations, he called them to Islam in their own languages. Remarkably, Sulayman was also given the extraordinary gift of understanding the languages of animals and birds! He could communicate with them, as demonstrated in his conversations with the ant and the hoopoe bird.

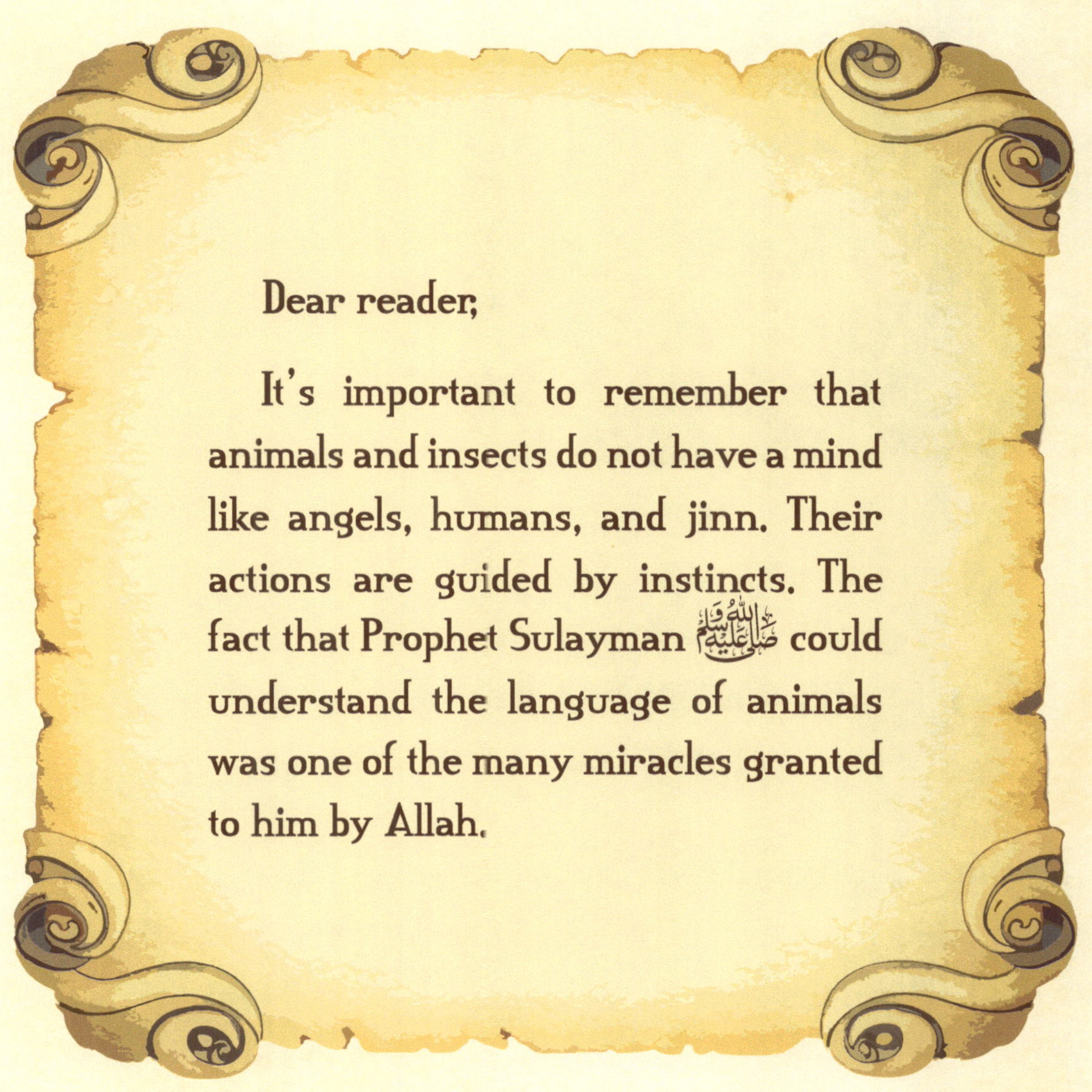

Dear reader,

It's important to remember that animals and insects do not have a mind like angels, humans, and jinn. Their actions are guided by instincts. The fact that Prophet Sulayman ﷺ could understand the language of animals was one of the many miracles granted to him by Allah.

Prophet Sulayman ﷺ and the Ant

One day, Prophet Sulayman was leading his army, which included jinn, humans and birds, on a campaign. As they traveled, they reached a valley inhabited by ants. When the army drew near, the queen of the ants said: "Oh, ants! Hurry into your homes so that

Sulayman and his soldiers do not trample you without noticing!"

Upon hearing the queen's ant warning, Sulayman smiled and thanked Allah for this unique gift, the understanding of animals' language. Out of compassion, he ordered his army to stop, giving the ants time to retreat to safety.

The story of Sulayman ﷺ and Bilqis, the Queen of Sheba

Prophet Sulayman ﷺ had a huge number of servants and subordinates, each assigned specific tasks. One of his trusted aides was the hoopoe bird, who was responsible for finding water for the Prophet and his army during their journeys. On one occasion, when the army was feeling thirsty, Sulayman noticed that the hoopoe was missing and warned that the birds would face consequences unless it had good reason for its absence.

When the hoopoe returned, it reported an intriguing discovery. It had seen a powerful and wealthy queen in the kingdom of Sheba. The queen, named Bilqis, had a magnificient golden throne decorated with various jewels and precious stones. However, she and her people worshiped the sun instead of Allah.

Prophet Sulayman ﷺ wrote a letter to queen Bilqis, inviting her to accept Islam and submit to his rule. The hoopoe delivered this letter to Bilqis' palace. After reading the letter, she informed her subjects about its content. She consulted with her advisors and decided to send Sulayman a gift, hoping to gauge his intentions and strength. She sent a delegation with numerous ornaments and jewels to test him.

When the gifts were presented to Prophet Sulayman, he did not accept them. Instead, he reminded the delegation that Allah had blessed him with far greater strength and power than what they had offered. He warned them if they did not submit, he would send an army against them that they would be unable to resist.

The Throne of Bilqis

When Queen Bilqis' envoys returned to her, they reported on Sulayman's immense power and strength of his army. They also conveyed his refusal of the gifts and his warning of a military campaign. Realizing Sulayman's power, Bilqis decided to visit him herself to learn more about his message.

Before leaving, Balqis ordered her throne to be hidden behind seven gates, locked and guarded. The queen's throne was enormous—80 cubits in length and 40 cubits in width. Her throne was an intricately decorated piece, made of gold and silver, and adorned with precious stones, and supported by legs of emerald and pearls.

As she traveled toward Sulayman, he decided to show her the glory of Islam by having her throne brought to his palace before she arrived. He asked his assembly if anyone could bring it to him. A powerful jinn offered to do so within half a day, but then a righteous man named Asif ibn Barkhiya, known for his piety and knowledge of the scriptures, said he could bring it in the blink of an eye. Instantly, the throne appeared before Sulayman, who praised Allah for this miraculous sign.

Balqis traveled with a grand delegation to meet Sulayman ﷺ. Prophet Sulayman ﷺ built for Bilqis a great palace, all made of glass, in the passages and above the ceiling of which water flowed, and fish and other aquatic inhabitants swam in it so that it seemed to the beholder that he was standing in a mass of water.

Sulayman wanted to show Bilqis proof of his power so that she would embrace Islam. He wanted her to see something that she had never seen in her life. He decided to deliver her throne to his palace as a clear proof of his prophecy, because she left the throne in her

palace under great guard.

When Bilqis arrived, she saw powerful evidence and obvious miracles. She was amazed! She thought that the glass floor is waves of water. When she saw her throne, she was amazed by the clear signs of Sulayman's prophethood. Sulayman had instructed that the throne be slightly altered to see if Bilqis would recognize it. When she was asked, "Is this your throne?" Bilqis, being very wise, replied, "It is as if it is."

Impressed by the signs and miracles she witnessed, Bilqis accepted Islam and abandoned the worship of the sun. She returned to Sheba and ruled her people with justice and faith in Allah.

Death of Prophet Sulayman ﷺ

Prophet Sulayman ﷺ lived for only 52 years, dedicating his entire life to the spread Islam. When he passed away, Allah concealed his death from the jinn who were working under his command. Sulayman died standing, leaning on his staff, and remained in this position for an entire year. The jinn continued their work, thinking that he was still alive, as they feared punishment if they disobeyed.

Prophets' bodies do not decompose, so there was no outward sign that Sulayman had passed away. It was only after a termite gnawed through his staff, causing his body to collapse, that the jinn realized he had been dead for a long time. This event was an obvious proof that the jinn do not have knowledge of the unseen. If they knew that Sulayman was dead, they would not have continued their hard labor for an entire year.

PROPHET ZAKARIYYĀ (ZECHARIAH) ﷺ

Prophet Zakariyya was a descendant of Prophet Sulayman ﷺ. He was a carpenter who earned his living through honest work, never seeking luxury or wealth. Like all prophets, Zakariyya dedicated his life to calling people to worship Allah and fulfilled his mission with patience and integrity, passing every test that Allah sent his way.

During his time, the ruler in Palestine was a tyrant and an arrogant man named Herod (Herodus) who oppressed the people, making life difficult for the Israelites. However, by the Grace of Allah, Prophet Zakariyya became a leader among his people, providing them with relief and guidance during these challenging times.

Raising Maryam

Maryam (Mary) was the daughter of a pious man from the descendants of Israel named 'Imran who was a leader and a teacher among the Israelites. His wife, a devout woman prayed earnestly for a child and made a vow to dedicate the child to the service of the mosque in Jerusalem.

However, before Maryam was born,' Imran passed away. When Maryam's mother gave birth, she found herself in a dilemma, as she had expected a son to fulfill her vow, but Allah blessed her with a daughter. Despite this, she wrapped Maryam in a cloth and took her to the mosque, leaving her in the care of the scholars, who were descendants of Harun (Aaron).

The scholars, knowing that Maryam's father had been their Imam, competed over who would have the honor of raising her. They casted lots, and by Allah's will, the responsibility fell to Prophet Zakariyya. Prophet Zakariyya and his wife, who was the sister of Maryam's mother, lovingly took care of Maryam, raising her with great care and devotion.

As Maryam grew older, extraordinary events began to occur. She lived in a secluded room at Al-Aqsa Mosque, dedicating herself to worship. Prophet Zakariyya would visit her and was amazed to find that she had fresh fruits out of the season—summer fruits in winter and winter fruits in summer—extraordinarily provided by Allah. Any extraordinary event that Allah grants to some of his pious people is called "Karamah".

The Du'a of Prophet Zakariyya for Offspring

As time passed, Prophet Zakariyya, longed for a child of his own. Though he was elderly and his wife was barren, he knew that nothing was impossible to Allah. He prayed to Allah, asking for a pious son who would carry on his mission of guiding the people of Israel after his death.

Zakariyya feared that if no righteous heir was left after him, his people might fall under the influence of corrupt relatives. Allah, who created Adam without parents, could certainly grant a child to elderly parents. Allah answered Zakariyya's sincere prayers and blessed him and his wife with a son, Yahya (John), even though Zakariyya was 99 years old and his wife was 98.

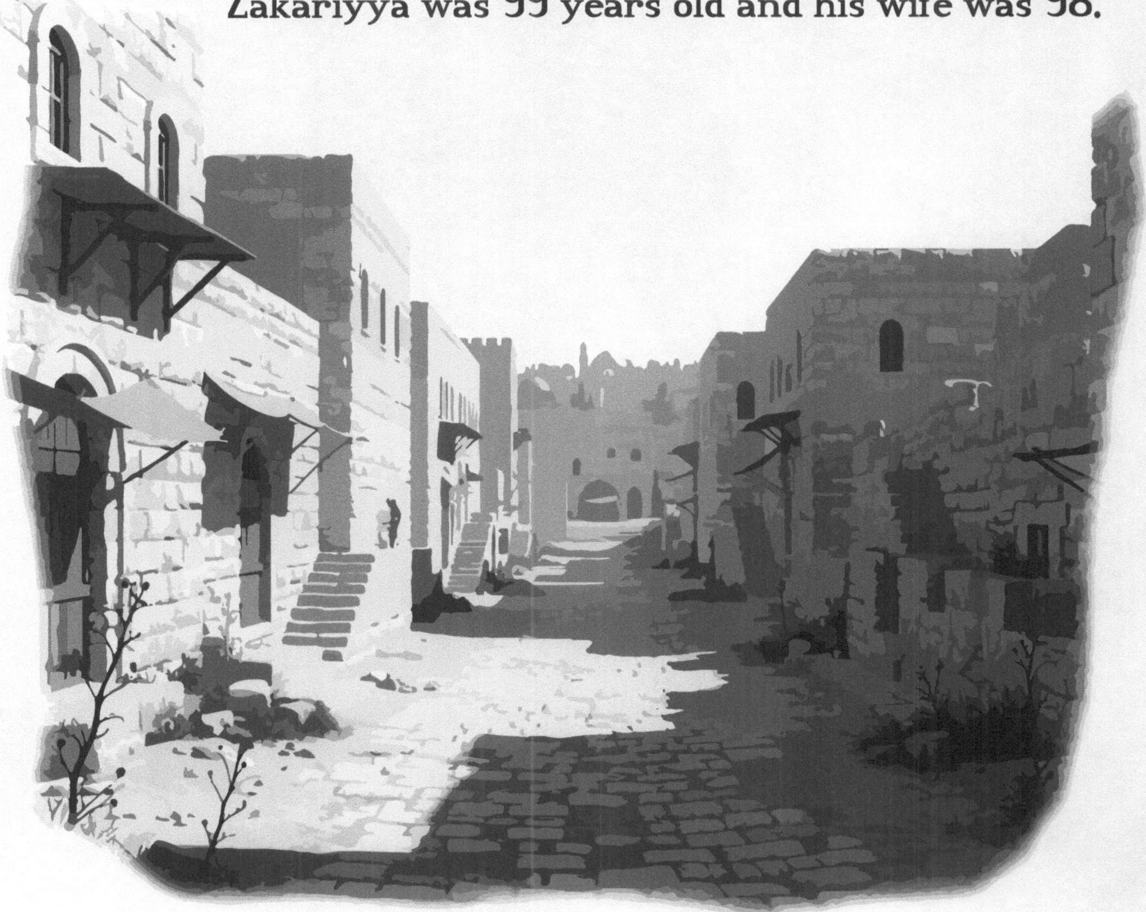

The Murder of Prophet Zakariyya

Despite the wisdom, kindness, and guidance that Prophet Zakariyya offered to the people of Israel, some among them turned against him. He was killed by some of his own people. After Maryam gave birth to ' Isa (Jesus), certain people falsely accused her and a carpenter named Yusuf of adultery. Others slandered Prophet Zakariyya, claiming that he committed immoral acts with Maryam.

As the situation escalated, Zakariyya was pursued by those who sought to kill him. In one account, it is said that the ruler of Palestine, Herod, ordered Zakariyya's death. Zakariyya fled from his pursuers and sought refuge in a garden. By Allah's will, a tree in the garden opened up, allowing Zakariyya to hide inside. The tree closed around him concealing him completely.

However, the devil, Iblees, appeared to the pursuers and pointed out the tree where Prophet Zakariyya was hiding. The evil men then cut the tree, killing Prophet Zakariyya in the process. Zakariyya's steadfastness in the face of persecution and his ultimate martyrdom are an example of patience, faith, and unwavering dedication to the truth.

PROPHET YAHYA (JOHN) 

Birth and Youth of Yahya

Prophet Yahya was the blessed son of Prophet Zakariyya and the maternal cousin of ʻIsa (Jesus). Yahya's birth was itself not an ordinary event, as his parents were elderly and childless. Prophet Zakariyya had prayed fervently for a son who would carry on the mission of spreading Allah's message. Allah revealed to Zakariyya that he will be given a son named Yahya, a name that had never been given before.

Even as a child, Yahya displayed wisdom and knowledge far beyond his years. Unlike other children, he displayed exceptional level of piety and compassion. When other children invited him to play, he responded, "We were not created for play." He treated everyone, whether family or strangers, with kindness. As he grew older, Yahya received revelation and became a prophet.

Yahya and his cousin 'Isa grew up together, sharing a bond of brotherhood and friendship. They were around the same age and were remarkably similar in righteousness and devotion to Allah. Yahya devoted his time to studying the Torah alongside Prophet 'Isa. Together, they recited, reflected, and mastered the teachings of the Holy Book with remarkable speed and insight.

Yahya and Isa lived simple lives; they had no wealth or homes of their own. They slept wherever night found them, content with their spiritual riches rather than earthly luxuries.

They subsided on whatever nature provided of raw vegetables and plants. Yahya was so dedicated to his mission that he had no desire for the luxuries of life. His heart was filled with love for Allah.

Yahya was also the first to follow Prophet 'Isa's call to spread Islam.

Herod and the Murder of Prophet Yahya

The ruler of Palestine at the time was Herod (Herodus). Initially, Herod had a good relationship with Prophet Yahya, often seeking his advice and being satisfied with his guidance. However, Herod was married to a woman who, as she aged, became increasingly insecure about losing her status and luxury. Fearing that Herod might replace her with a younger wife, she concocted a devious plan. She dressed her daughter from a previous marriage with the finest clothes, and brought her to Herod, urging him to marry her. However, this girl was Herod's stepdaughter, and such a marriage was forbidden in the revealed law.

Herod hesitated and consulted Prophet Yahya, who firmly declared that such a marriage was forbidden by Allah. His answer enraged Herod's wife, who saw Yahya as an obstacle to her plans. She became determined to have Yahya killed, manipulating Herod by appealing to his desires and insecurities.

At first, Herod resisted the idea of killing Yahya, knowing that killing a prophet was a grievous sin, an apostasy. However, under relentless pressure from this evil woman, he eventually gave in to her demands. Tragically, Prophet Yahya was executed while he was praying. His head was brought to Herod as a gruesome trophy meant to satisfy the desires of the wicked. But the blood of Yahya, a Prophet of Allah, continued to boil as a sign of the terrible injustice committed by Herod and his court.

Retribution for Injustice

Herod believed that by killing Yahya, he would demonstrate his power and strength, while his wife hoped to secure her luxurious lifestyle. But both were terribly wrong. By the Will of Allah, retribution soon followed.

Herod's wife met a gruesome end when she fell from the roof of the place and was attacked by dogs that tore her apart. As for Herod, Allah inflicted Bakhtanassar, a ruler from Babylon, upon him to punish him and his followers. Bakhtanassar's army swept through Palestine, defeating him and his forces, bringing an end to his tyrannical rule.

There are different accounts about the final place of Prophet Yahya. Some scholars believe that his head is buried in the Umayyad mosque in Damascus, while others say that his hand is buried in Sidon, where a beautiful maqam (shrine) stands today.

PROPHET 'ĪSĀ (JESUS) 

Maryam, the Daughter of 'Imran

Maryam (the Virgin Mary), the daughter of 'Imran, came from the noble lineage of Prophet Dawud. Her father passed away before her birth, but her pious mother ensured that Maryam was raised in the best way, teaching her to be devoted to Allah. Prophet Zakariyya took care of Maryam at Al-Aqsa mosque, where she grew up pure and free from sins. Maryam dedicated much of her time to worshipping Allah and became known for her deep piety and, at an early age she became a waliyyah (a saint), a righteous pious Muslim. Allah blessed her with extraordinary matters, such as providing her with fruits that were out of season. Maryam is the best woman of all times.

Maryam's Immaculate Conception

One day, while Maryam was worshipping in a quiet place in the eastern part of the mosque, she was surprised by the appearance of a handsome young man. In reality, this was Angel Gabriel who had taken the form of a man. Frightened, Maryam moved away from him and said, "If you fear God, then do not harm me."

Gabriel reassured her saying, "I am the messenger of your Lord, sent to give you a pure boy." Maryam was astonished and asked, "How can I have a child if no man has touched me?"

Gabriel replied, "This is what your Lord decreed. Creating a child without a father is easy for Allah. He will be a sign for the people and a mercy from Allah." Gabriel then fulfilled the order of Allah and blew the soul of 'Isa into Maryam through the collar of her dress. Thus the Virgin Mary conceived immaculately.

The Birth of Prophet 'Isa

As the time for the birth of her son drew near, Maryam became deeply worried about how her people would react. Knowing that she has no husband and expecting a child, she feared they would accuse her of dishonor and question her integrity, as well as that of Prophet Zakariyya, who had cared for her.

To avoid their blame, Maryam withdrew to a secluded place. As she leaned against the trunk of a dried palm tree, the pain of labor began. Overwhelmed by her situation and in her distress, she wished she could disappear, dreading the thought of facing her people with a newborn.

But in her moment of greatest hardship, Allah provided relief. Angel Gabriel appeared once again and comforted her. He told her not to be sad and reminded her that Allah's support was with her. Gabriel then pointed to a small stream that had appeared beneath her, providing her with fresh water. He also instructed her to shake the trunk of the dried palm tree, and extraordinarily, the tree became green again, and soft, ripe dates fell down for her to eat.

Gabriel told Maryam to eat the dates and drink from the stream, so she could regain her strength after childbirth and advised her to vow silence for a day when she returned to her people, as was allowed in the revealed laws of the time to abstain from talking like we abstain from food while fasting, protecting her from their immediate questioning. Feeling comforted and strengthened by Allah's support, Maryam prepared to return to her people, cradling her newborn son, 'Isa, in her arms.

The Childhood and Youth of Prophet ʻIsa

When Maryam returned to her people carrying a baby, they were very shocked and some began accusing her of wrongdoing. Without speaking, Maryam simply pointed to her son, signaling them to speak to him. Angered, they thought she was mocking them. Then something extraordinary happened—Baby ʻIsa, only 40 days old, spoke! Allah gave him the ability to speak to defend his mother from their false accusations and prove her innocence. After that extraordinary moment, he grew up like any other child, speaking at the usual age.

At that time, the cruel ruler Herod heard about the birth of a remarkable boy in Bethlehem. Fearing for her son's safety, Lady Maryam traveled with ʻIsa to Egypt, where he received his early education and learned to write. After some time, they returned to Palestine and settled in Nazareth.

سورة مريم

قَالَ إِنِّي عَبْدُ اللَّهِ آتَانِيَ الْكِتَابَ وَجَعَلَنِي نَبِيًّا ﴿٧٢﴾
وَجَعَلَنِي مُبَارَكًا أَيْنَ مَا كُنتُ وَأَوْصَانِي بِالصَّلَاةِ وَالزَّكَاةِ
مَا دُمْتُ حَيًّا ﴿٧٢﴾ وَبَرًّا بِوَالِدَتِي وَلَمْ يَجْعَلْنِي جَبَّارًا شَقِيًّا ﴿٧٢﴾
وَالسَّلَامُ عَلَيَّ يَوْمَ وُلِدتُّ وَيَوْمَ أَمُوتُ وَيَوْمَ أُبْعَثُ حَيًّا ﴿٧٢﴾

The Physical Appearance of Prophet 'Isa

Like all prophets, 'Isa was blessed with a beautiful appearance. He had a complexion that was neither very white nor very dark, with a slight reddish or brownish tone. His hair was black and straight, and he was of above-average height with a strong, handsome built.

The Mission of Prophet 'Isa ﷺ

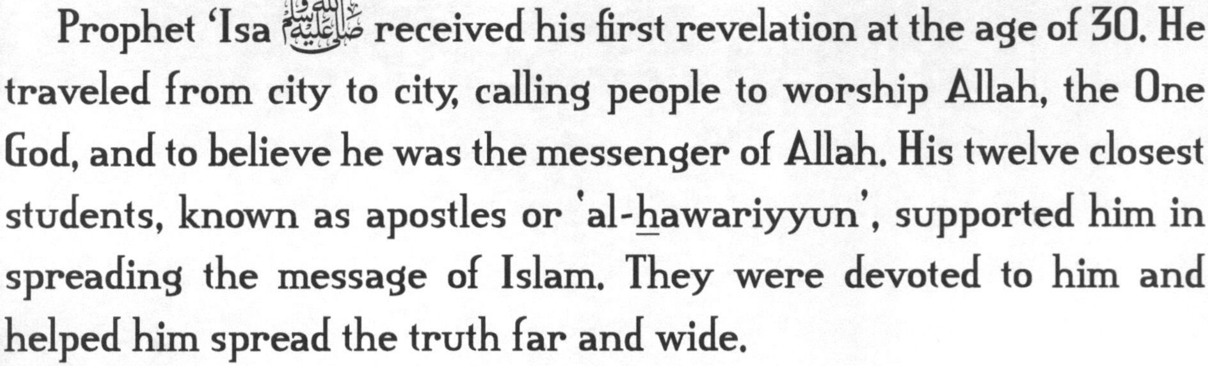

Prophet 'Isa ﷺ received his first revelation at the age of 30. He traveled from city to city, calling people to worship Allah, the One God, and to believe he was the messenger of Allah. His twelve closest students, known as apostles or 'al-hawariyyun', supported him in spreading the message of Islam. They were devoted to him and helped him spread the truth far and wide.

'Isa said:
"Worship Allah, the Only God, do not attribute a partner to Him and believe that I am the Messenger of Allah."

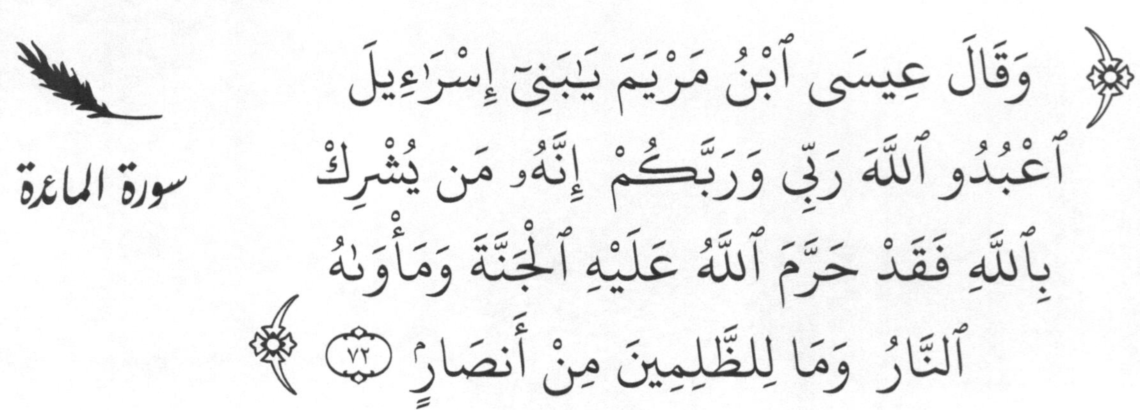

Prophet ʻIsa lived a very modest life. He had no home of his own and slept wherever night found him. His diet was simple, consisting of raw plants like dandelions leaves and Jew's mallow (molokhia). He wore clothing made of unwoven wool. Like all the prophets, ʻIsa's hearts was not attached to the worldly matters, his focus was always on the worship of Allah and spreading his message.

Miracles of Prophet ʻIsa ﷺ

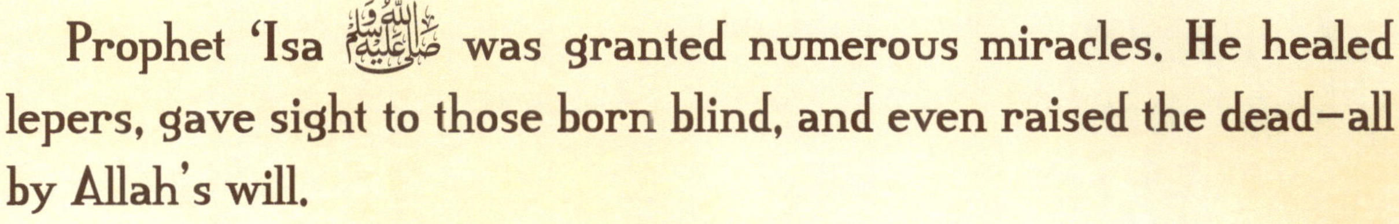

Prophet ʻIsa ﷺ was granted numerous miracles. He healed lepers, gave sight to those born blind, and even raised the dead—all by Allah's will.

The Miracle of the Dyed Cloth: All Colors from One

One of his first miracles happened when his mother, Maryam, sent him to learn various professions. ‘Isa once worked at a place where they dyed clothes. One day, the owner, before leaving on a trip, instructed ‘Isa ﷺ: "I have cloths to be dyed in different colors. I have attached a thread of the right color to each item, so be sure to match them accordingly." ‘Isa ﷺ heated a large vat, mixed paints of different colors, and placed all the cloths in the vat together. He then said, "Become, by the Will of Allah, what I demand."

When the owner returned, he saw all the clothes in the vat and feared they are ruined. But, to his astonishment, when ‘Isa began taking the items out, each one was perfectly dyed in the correct color, just as the owner had intended. Realizing this was a sign from Allah, the owner became a believer and a follower of Prophet ‘Isa ﷺ.

The Miracle with the Fishermen

Prophet ‘Isa ﷺ once passed by fishermen, one of whom was in charge and named Sham‘un. When ‘Isa asked what they are doing, they replied, "We are fishing." Prophet ‘Isa ﷺ then asked, "Would you like to join me in calling people to the path of Allah? "They asked, "Who are you?" He responded, "I am 'Isa, the son of Maryam, the slave of Allah and messenger of Allah." The fishermen asked for proof. Knowing that Sham'un had not caught any fish that night, Prophet 'Isa instructed him to cast his net into the water again. 'Isa read a du'a, and after a few moments passed, the net was filled with so many fish that it almost broke, and Sham'un had to call for help from another boat. Amazed, the fishermen believed in the message of Prophet 'Isa ﷺ, left fishing, and followed him.

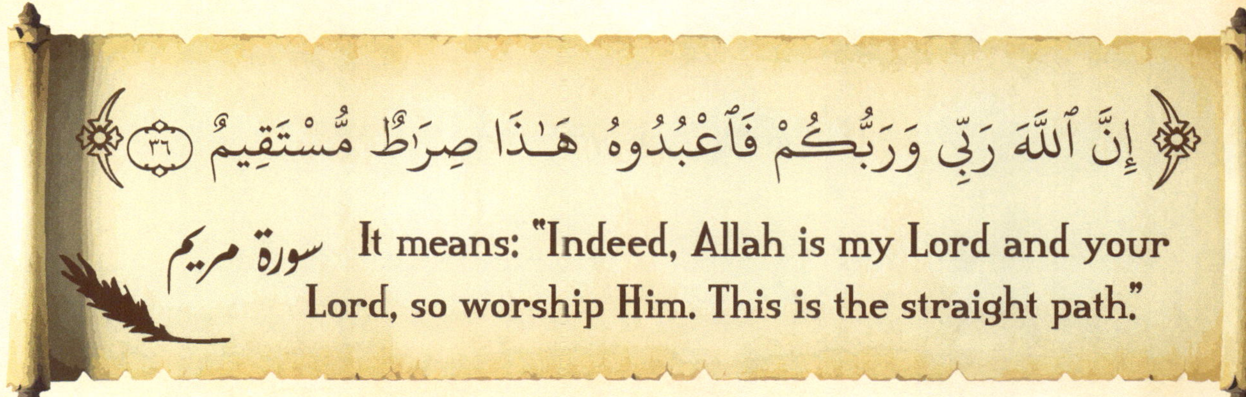

The Clay Bat

On another occasion, some people challenged prophet 'Isa to produce a bat out of clay and make it fly. Prophet 'Isa shaped a bat from clay, blew on it with trust in Allah, and by Allah's Will, the bat came to life and flew into the sky. When the bat flew out of sight, it fell lifeless.

People asked to make a bat because it is one of the most fascinating creatures. It flies without feathers, does not lay eggs like a bird but instead gives birth like an animal and nurses her young with milk like other mammals.

Healing the Blind

Prophet ʻIsa ﷺ also cured those who were blind or suffering from leprosy—a disease that repelled most people, as they feared contagion and was incurable at the time. Despite the advanced medical knowledge of that era, no doctor could cure these conditions. However, Prophet ʻIsa healed the blind with a touch and cured lepers by Allah's command.

Bringing the Dead to Life

Moreover, Prophet ʻIsa ﷺ performed the extraordinary miracle of raising the dead. One such miracle involved his friend, ʻAzar. When ʻAzar fell ill, his sister sent for Prophet ʻIsa, but by the time he arrived, ʻAzar had already died and was buried. ʻIsa went to his grave, read a duʻa and called out, "Get up, by the Will of Allah." By the Will of Allah, ʻAzar rose from the grave, lived for many years, and even had children.

Another miracle involved a man who had died leaving his

elderly mother heartbroken. As the man was being carried on a stretcher to his grave, Prophet 'Isa ﷺ prayed for him, and by the Will of Allah, the man came back to life, stood up, took the stretcher and walked home.

People who envied prophet 'Isa's miracles tried to challenge him further. They demanded he raise Sam, the son of Prophet Noah, from the dead, believing it would be impossible since Sam had died long time ago. Prophet 'Isa ﷺ asked them to show him his grave, prayed to Allah, and Sam emerged from his grave, confirming that 'Isa was indeed the messenger of Allah by pointing to 'Isa and saying." Believe him, he is a prophet", before returning to his rest. Despite witnessing this, some people refused to believe and accused Prophet 'Isa of sorcery.

Another miracle of Prophet 'Isa ﷺ was his ability to inform people what they ate, stored in their homes, and saved for the next day.

The Book of Prophet 'Isa ﷺ

Prophet 'Isa ﷺ was given Al-Injeel, a divine book revealed in the Syriac language. Along with the Injeel, Prophet 'Isa brought a new set of laws (Shari'ah) that differed in some rulings from those of the Torah. At that time, the Torah was still unaltered, and 'Isa studied it in his youth. However, over time, both the Torah and the Injeel were distorted. The versions of the Injeel and Torah that exist today are not the original ones revealed to Jesus or Moses and contain many contradictions and fabrications.

Jesus foretold of the coming of another Prophet after him, whose name would be Ahmad—one of the names of Prophet Muhammad ﷺ. He advised his followers to believe in this final prophet when he appeared.

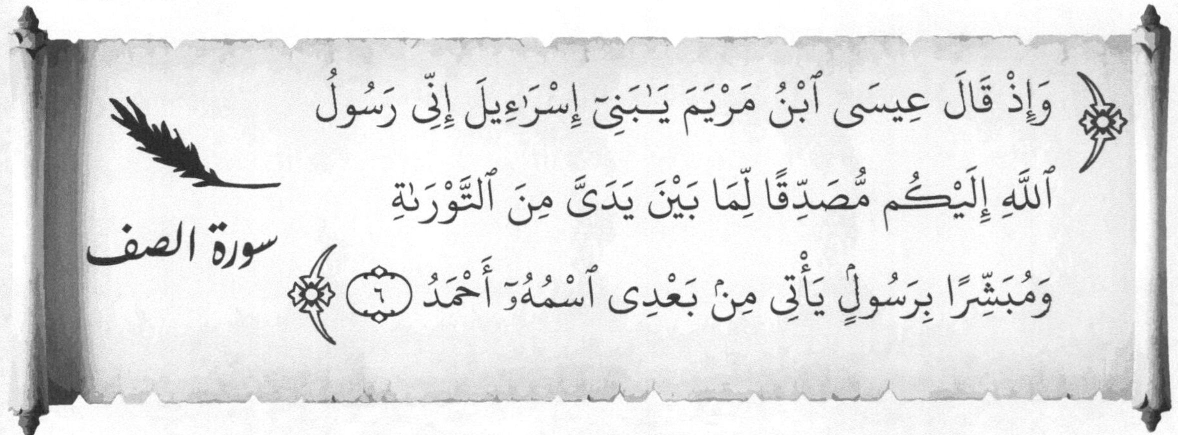

The Plot to kill Prophet 'Isa ﷺ

Prophet 'Isa steadfastly continued his mission to guide the people, but the unbelievers grew increasingly threatened by his influence. They feared losing power and control. Among them were some from Bani Israel, who claimed to follow Prophet Musa but disbelieved when they refused to accept Prophet's 'Isa's message. They conspired to kill him.

The Martyr Who Took His Place

Allah revealed their evil plan to Prophet Jesus ﷺ, so 'Isa gathered twelve of his closest companions and asked, "Who among you is willing to take on my appearance, be killed in my place, and be my companion in Paradise?" The youngest companion eagerly volunteered, but prophet 'Isa asked him to sit. When Prophet 'Isa asked again, the young man stood up once more and said, "Me." After the third time, Prophet ʻIsa said, "It is you."

By Allah's will, this companion took on the appearance of Prophet ʻIsa. Meanwhile, Prophet ʻIsa was lifted to the heavens through a small window in the roof of the house, at the age of thirty-three (33). When the conspirators broke into the house, they seized the young companion, believing him to be ʻIsa, and killed him. He became a martyr, enjoying an honored status in the Hereafter. As for Prophet ʻIsa, he was saved from their plot, neither killed nor crucified.

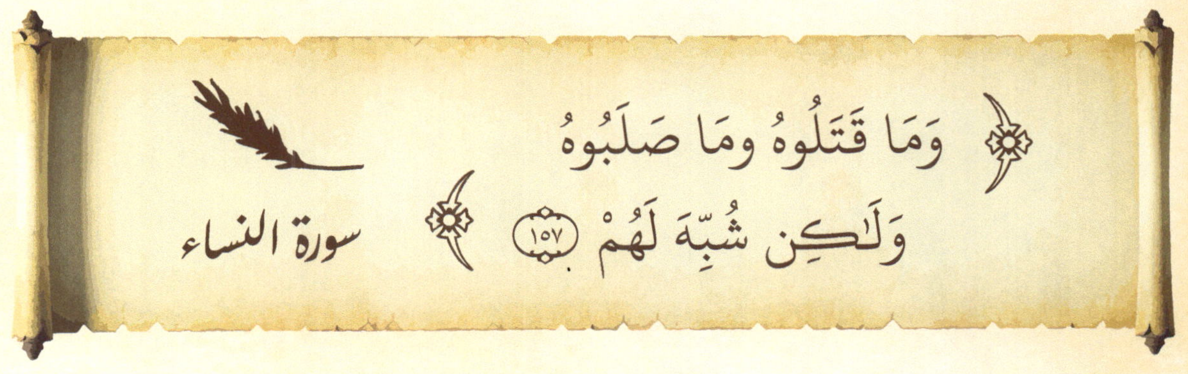

Return of Prophet 'Isa to Earth 

Prophet 'Isa is still alive in the second heaven, where he worships Allah without the need to eat or drink, much like angels. Allah, the Creator of all things, sustains him. Although more than two thousand years have passed, Allah has preserved Prophet 'Isa's life.

One of the greatest signs of the approaching Day of Judgment is the return of 'Isa to the Earth. Accompanied by two angels, he will descend from the second heaven to Earth, near a white lighthouse in Eastern Damascus and rule with justice. For forty years, peace will spread across the land. The Earth will reveal its treasures, poverty will vanish, and even the animals will be in harmony. The wolf will walk next to the flock of sheep without attacking them, a sign of the prevailing justice and universal peace.

At this time, there will be no unbelievers. All humans will be Muslims; the unbelievers will die

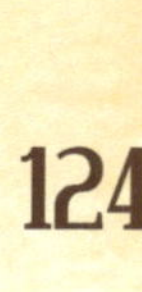

with the breath of Jesus. Jesus will break the cross and kill the pig, a confirmation that he is ruling with the laws revealed to the last prophet, Muhammad, and as a proof that he did not tell people to worship him nor to eat pig, affirming the truth of his message and rejecting false beliefs attributed to him.

During his time on Earth, Prophet ‘Isa will visit the grave of Prophet Muhammad and offer his Salam. Some scholars said he will marry and have children, though Allah knows best. After his time on Earth ends, Prophet ‘Isa will die and be buried in Medina, besides Prophet Muhammad ﷺ.

A Legacy of Truth

After Prophet ‘Isa's ascension, his followers remained steadfast on the Religion of Islam for many years. However over time, their number dwindled, and distortions of his teachings emerged. Pagan practices spread, and some people began to worship ‘Isa and his mother, Maryam, despite the clear message he brought. True believers, those who held firm to his teachings, faced persecution. They fled to remote isolated areas such as the mountains, living in caves and surviving on plant foods to protect their faith. The last true follower of Prophet ‘Isa passed away five years before Prophet Muhammad received revelation, leaving Muhammad as the only believer amongst the people until Prophet Muhammad ﷺ renewed the call and the mission of the prophets.

The Prophets' Legacy & the Most Noble Mission

From the time of Adam to the time of Prophet Muhammad ﷺ, Allah sent a succession of prophets with the most noble mission: to guide humanity to the truth. Each prophet brought light and wisdom to people and called them to righteousness. This noble mission was passed down through the prophets, from Adam to Idrees, from Noah to Abraham, from Moses to Jesus, and finally to Muhammad ﷺ, who completed the message for all of humanity.

Prophet Jesus's ﷺ life and his return are a reminder that truth will always prevail, no matter how much it is opposed or forgotten. As Muslims, we honor and love all prophets, following their example and upholding the truth of their message.

May we always be inspired by their courage and dedication to the most noble mission of all—guiding humanity to the worship of Allah alone and spreading goodness. May we be among those who remain steadfast in the face of challenges and carry the light of faith forward.

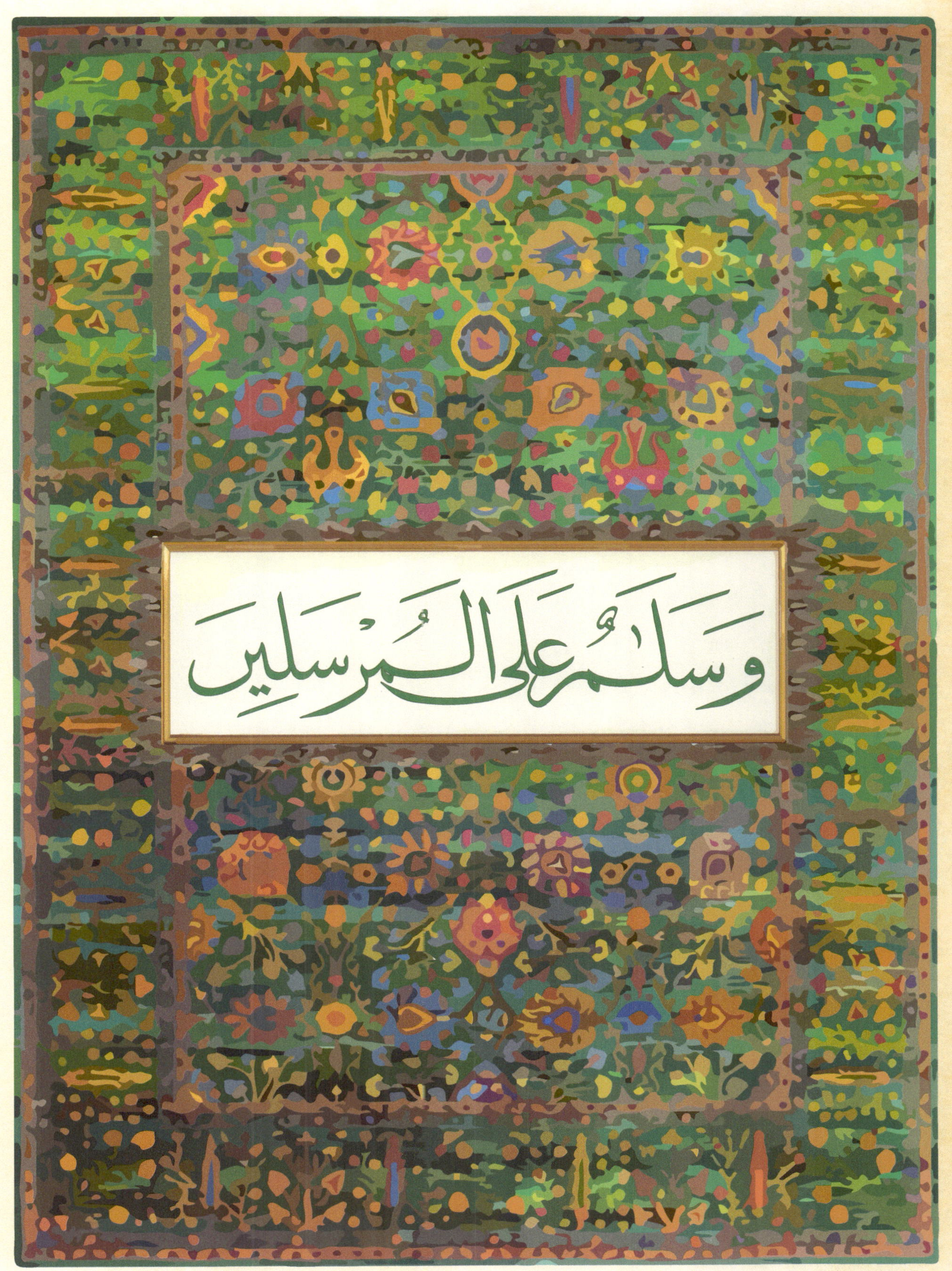
وسلم على المرسلين

EPILOGUE

Dear reader,

As we reach the end of these stories, we are reminded of the great blessing of following the path of the noble prophets and their mission. Being a believer is the greatest gift in this life. Though life is full of challenges, Allah provides a way for the righteous to overcome difficulties, as we've seen throughout this book.

So, my young friend, strive for piety and knowledge. This will open new horizons for you. Remember the stories of the Prophets often. Reflect on how they faced their trials with courage, and think about how you would act if one of them were beside you.

If you ever forget the lessons learned here, return to this book, and the journey through the lives of the prophets will begin again!

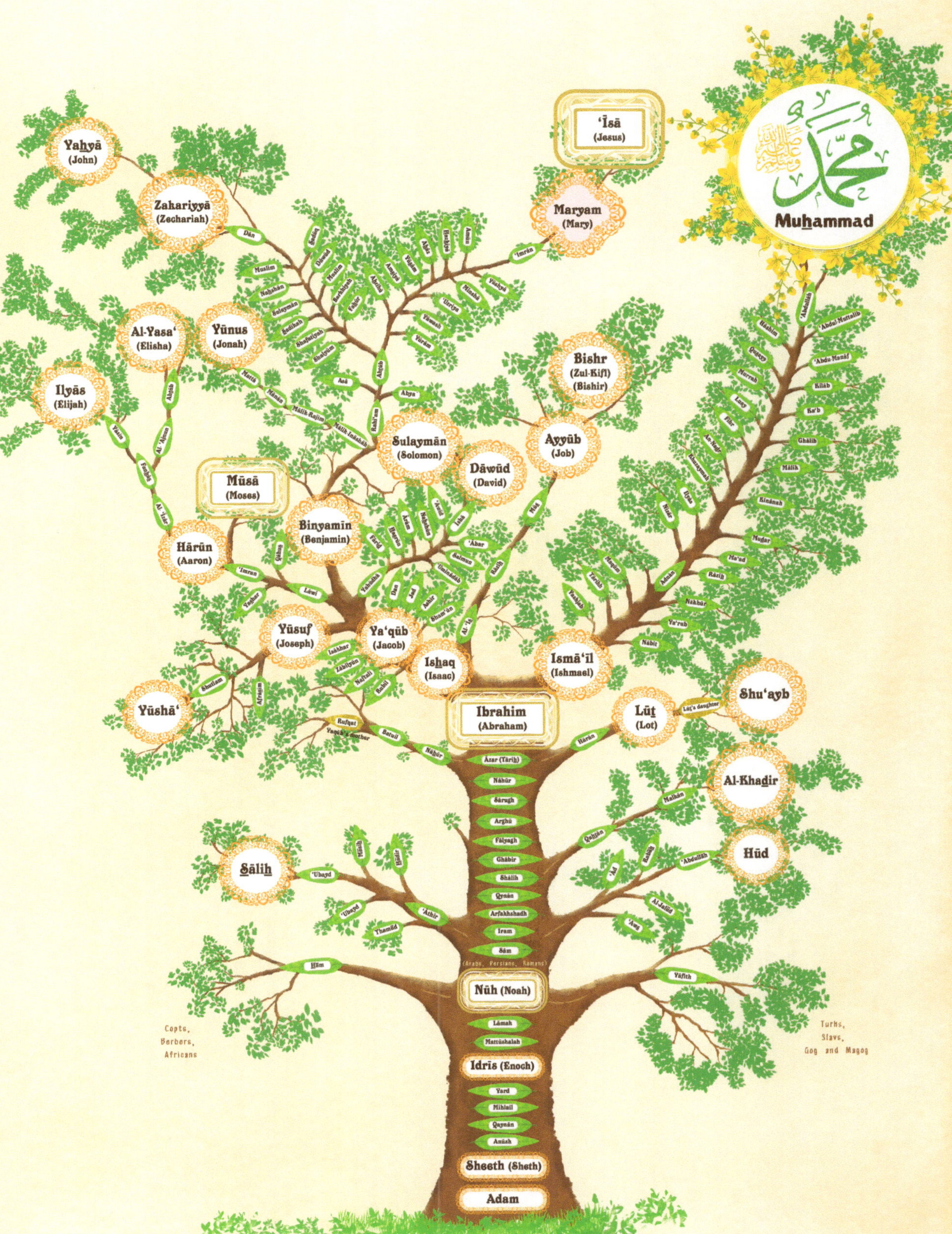
Muhammad
'Īsā (Jesus)
Maryam (Mary)
Yahyā (John)
Zakariyyā (Zechariah)
Al-Yasa' (Elisha)
Yūnus (Jonah)
Ilyās (Elijah)
Bishr (Zul-Kifl) (Bishir)
Sulaymān (Solomon)
Dāwūd (David)
Ayyūb (Job)
Mūsā (Moses)
Hārūn (Aaron)
Binyamin (Benjamin)
Yūsuf (Joseph)
Ya'qūb (Jacob)
Ishaq (Isaac)
Ismā'īl (Ishmael)
Yūshā'
Ibrahim (Abraham)
Lūt (Lot)
Shu'ayb
Al-Khadir
Hūd
Sālih
Āzar (Tārih)
Nāhūr
Sārugh
Arghū
Fālyagh
Ghābir
Shālih
Qynān
Arfakhshadh
Iram
Sām
(Arabs, Persians, Romans)
Hām
Yāfith
Nūh (Noah)
Lāmak
Mattūshalah
Idrīs (Enoch)
Yard
Mihlail
Qaynān
Anūsh
Sheeth (Sheth)
Adam
Copts, Berbers, Africans
Turks, Slavs, Gog and Magog